HOW TO RETIRE HAPPY

Planning the Ultimate
Retirement Lifestyle

GUY BURBERRY

WHY READ THIS BOOK?

A RETIRED CLIENT recently got invited to a lunch with some of her former co-workers She described it as a nice reunion with lots of laughs shared, but midway through the meal, the tone of the conversation changed.

Finally, one of her old co-workers looked at their friends and said, "I'll ask her."

"Ask me what?" my client responded.

"Tell us and be honest. Do you regret it?

"Regret what?"

"Retiring," her friend responded.

Without skipping a beat, my client responded, "Not for a second!"

The ladies had a lot of questions, but "How did you know you were ready?" was at the top of their list.

Recent retirees, especially those who retired young, report the most common question they receive is, "What do you do with your time?" If you're like most people, you probably have a lot of questions yourself. Chances are you picked this book up because you are experiencing many of these same doubts.

Over the next six chapters, I will lead you through a process to help you identify your personal barriers to retiring and design a retirement plan that is specific to your goals. In the accompanying workbook, I will ask follow-up questions and provide further guidance to ensure that your retirement plan allows you to enjoy the life you've always dreamed of having. Be sure to make notes at the end of each chapter so that you can create your personal dream plan for retirement.

In Chapter 1, we will begin by outlining the mechanical aspects of retiring, beyond the strictly financial. **What do you need to accomplish in the years leading up to your retirement?** I will spur you into action mode by providing examples of what other successful retirees do to get ready for this milestone. Retirement is yet another phase in the journey we call life, and the people who seem to have it all together for this transition always have a plan. They set goals and put their plan in motion. I'll get you thinking about where you want to live, what tools you need for your chosen day-to-day activities, and what aspects of your life are best tended to while you are still earning active income.

In Chapter 2, we will work together to identify **your retirement personality**. Identifying the retirement personality, or personalities, that resonate with you and your goals will make you better equipped to fully enjoy your leisure time. Once you get your mind wrapped around what you truly desire, you can take the steps necessary to put your plan in motion. Not everyone wants the same things for their retirement and some people have obstacles they need to overcome. But an important part of not feeling lost in your free time is coming to terms with your retirement personality.

From there, you need to get your creative juices flowing. **How will you occupy the time you used to devote to work and work-related activities?** This is a common struggle, and Chapter 3 presents a lengthy list of suggestions so that you can identify at least one or two activities that align with your interests. You don't want to simply retire from something but rather to something. This is a theme that we will explore throughout the book. It is important to keep this in mind as you plan to fill your days with pleasurable activities.

Life doesn't always go as planned, and many individuals get to a point when they feel the need to retire but haven't managed to save as much as they'd hoped. All is not lost. I have devoted Chapter 4 to helping you **create extra income out of your hobbies and interests**. This chapter is packed with suggestions to get you on your way to retirement while filling any financial gaps.

Retirement isn't just a permanent vacation. It's made up of several phases. In Chapter 5, we will delve into **the five typical phases a person goes through in retirement**. This is where I discuss the psychological aspects that often create challenges for individuals coming to terms with their imminent retirement. Trust me when I say that you are not alone in your feelings and concerns. I will offer solutions to help you navigate these phases and avoid spending too much time overthinking. My goal is to help you maximize the free time that you have worked so hard to achieve.

For the most part, people don't like change. It can be difficult to adjust and adapt. Sometimes success doesn't come from knowledge or experience as much as a willingness to adapt well to change. Its likely that you will experience feelings of loss as you move into another major phase of your life. That's why Chapter 6 identifies **the five typical losses people experience** as they undergo this transition. We will cover topics like loss of identity, loss of structure, loss of purpose, loss of relationships, and loss of power. I'll offer suggestions that empower you to navigate these losses in the best ways possible. My goal is to help you organize your thoughts in such a way that you come to the right solutions on your own.

By the end of this book, you will have gained a greater appreciation for what it takes to create the retirement lifestyle you have always dreamed of. My definition of success has always been to create and finance a life full of enriching experiences while maintaining happiness and peace of mind. It is my sincere goal that this guide provides you with the tools to achieve success in your own lives. As you navigate the chapters, the accompanying workbook will help you take notes on each section, prompting you with questions that will help you create your personal dream plan for retirement. Once you've got your plan in place, you can finally take the first step toward creating your own glorious retirement!

CHAPTER 1

PREPARING FOR RETIREMENT

WHILE THIS IS not a book on financial planning or saving for retirement, there are many things an individual or family may want to do before they retire. After 26 years working as a financial planner, one of my consistent observations has been that there some significant psychological barriers to retiring. When we meet someone new, the conversation always seems to lead to that pesky question: What do you do for a living? Our occupation is a big part of our identities, and the loss of this element is one of the major losses covered in Chapter 6. It's also a great place to start when beginning to prepare for retirement. What are you going to do?

One of the best ways to approach retirement is to decide to retire to something rather than simply from something. This phase of life is the culmination of decades of hard work, planning, and careful decision making. I have often said that wealth is built in $50 and $100 increments. Every year, we make a series of financial decisions. We decide what to purchase, how to purchase it, when to spend or save, when to upgrade to that new home or car, whether to save up or buy on credit. Most retirees are quite proud of the careful choices they have made throughout their lives, choices which have, in the end, afforded them this glorious opportunity.

So, step one is to really embrace this opportunity. There is nothing wrong with wearing it as a badge of honour. Especially if you retire at a young age, you may be met with some negative responses as certain people struggle to figure out why you're in a position to retire while they seem so far from achieving the same goal. Many retirees have reported to me that people often ask if they have given up, but the most common question by far is, "What do you do with your time?" A simple answer would be to suggest that they read this book. In the next several chapters, I will provide a road map for creating the North American dream and help you navigate the emotions and challenges you will likely encounter on your journey. There are some important steps we can take in the years leading up to retirement to help make our transition as smooth as possible.

Let's get started!

CREATING A PLAN

One of the number one reasons people struggle so much with retirement is that they haven't created a plan. When we are in high school, we are encouraged to devote time to career planning, and counsellors often work with students to help them decide how they want to earn money and guide them on how to get there. If you decided to get married, you likely had to plan some sort of wedding. You may have planned for your child's education by opening a RESP (Registered Education Savings Plan) and contributing to it over many years. Business owners often make a business plan every year to establish and achieve their career goals. If you are working toward retiring one day, you have already been planning your finances in order to make retirement a reality.

The point is that anyone who has achieved success in any area of their lives has devoted some time to creating a plan and carrying it out. Why would retirement be any different? This is why I created a workbook to assist you in this very task. At the end of each chapter, I encourage you to review the planning notes in this workbook. I have outlined specific questions aimed at helping you create your plan. By the end of Chapter 6, you will have a detailed draft of your retirement strategy. You may edit or adjust this plan many times as you journey through retirement, but once you have this first draft, all you need to do is take the first step to put your plan in motion. Having clearly identified objectives will help you meet your goals, clarify what you hope to accomplish, reduce the sense of loss that you may experience, and improve your overall satisfaction with retirement.

These notes will provide the framework for what you will do with your days. Throughout your work life, you are generally told what you need to accomplish to stay employed. If you were a business owner, you needed to create some sort of structure for yourself to successfully deliver your products or services and create an income. When you retire, you are in the business of creating a life full of enriching experiences for yourself, and what that looks like is entirely up to you. Your journey to creating your plan begins here.

WHERE WILL YOU LIVE?

This is a major decision and one that will likely be determined by the type of lifestyle you desire. In fact, where you decide to live may be in large part based on your retirement personality, which we will cover in Chapter 2. There are many ways retirees approach their living arrangements, so let's cover a few to get you thinking about which suits your personal needs and desired lifestyle.

WILL YOU RELOCATE?

The decision to relocate for retirement is a big one that carries many emotions. If you are the adventurous type, relocating to another country can seem exciting. If you find comfort in familiarity, that type of move may feel terrifying. Let's consider a couple of examples to outline some of the steps in the process and get you asking yourself the types of questions that help you determine if a move for retirement, is the right step for you and your family.

Where I reside in Southwestern Ontario, Canada, we often look forward to summer weekends in cottage country. Whether your family was fortunate enough to have their own cottage, you got invited to a friend's cottage, or you simply rented one for the weekend, it is a popular summer vacation spot. It is also a place many dream of relocating to after retirement. Cottage country is a nickname for a region predominantly in Central Ontario. Muskoka is a region two hours north of Toronto spanning 6,475 square kilometres, has some 1,600 lakes, and sees 2.1 million visitors annually. Populated with several villages, towns, and farming communities, the region draws people in with lakeside hotels and resorts near golf courses, country clubs, and marinas. All of this makes it a great vacation spot, as well as a popular place to relocate to during your golden years. For people who can brave the snowy

Canadian winters and dream of boating in the summer and snow-mobiling or ice fishing in winter, this can be a great spot to retire.

Panama is the only country in the world where you can watch the sun rise on the Pacific Ocean and set on the Atlantic Ocean. If the smell of salty sea air and the idea of escaping Canadian winters are more your speed, you may wish to investigate Panama's Pensionado Program. This program permits foreigners to seek legal residency if they have a verifiable minimum income of $1,000 USD per month for the rest of their lives. This income may come from a government program or private corporation back in one's home country. The program also carries many benefits and discounts that make enjoying retirement in one of the safest countries in Central America a reality within many retirees' budgets. A couple can live comfortably on a combined income of $3,000 per month while a single person can live comfortably on $1,400–$1,700 per month. Keep in mind that your lifestyle and residence location play a huge role in your budget. Benefits of the Pensionado Program include exemption from import tax for household goods, discounts on utility bills, loans, airline tickets and other transportation, and even home mortgages for personal residence. Discounts also include doctor's bills, dental and eye exams, medicines, cultural and sporting events, and hotels.

Panama is not the only desirable and affordable destination for today's retirees. A simple internet search will bring up dozens of articles on popular retirement locations, discussing their benefits and drawbacks. Deciding to relocate to another country is a huge decision and may take months or years of consideration. I recommend using a little vacation time to research your potential home-to-be well in advance of such a big decision.

Let's look at some of the metrics you may want to consider when determining whether one of these popular retirement destinations is right for you. When you look at lists of desirable retirement destinations, you may begin to realize that there are a lot of factors to consider beyond having enjoyed a vacation there.

While there are people for which money is no object, most retirees must consider what kind of lifestyle their nest egg will afford them. Cost of living and the affordability of lifestyle must factor into your decision-making process. Think about the activities you enjoy, the restaurants you frequent, and the things you cannot live without, then compare costs. For some households, this will quickly narrow your feasible options. Don't forget about costs related to housing and health care. Quality of life is a high priority for retirees. Do you prefer a fast-paced urban lifestyle with everything in close proximity or the peace and quiet of a small town or rural area? Consider whether your chosen destination provides the necessary elements for the life you've always dreamed of. Will you have easy access to your hobbies and interests? Consider the climate and proximity to resources. Do you enjoy winter activities or are you happier at the beach? Do you want to breathe that clean mountain air, or do you love fishing and boating and wish to be near a lake or river? Are there places that offer both?

Access to health care at an affordable price is also a big factor as we age. Whether it is during a trial period, or you are factoring it into your long-term coverage, international health insurance may be the safest and most reliable option for long-term global medical care. Especially if you choose to retire to a less developed country, local health care plans may not be available or desirable. Luckily, there is a lot of information available online, so you can research ahead of time and make your health care arrangements in advance. There is a reason that certain destinations, like Costa

Rica or Panama, become hot spots for North American expatriation. Access to quality health care is high on their list of priorities. Safety and low crime rates are things retirees often factor into their decision making as well.

It is always an excellent idea to do a trial run before purchasing land or buying a new home. Seeing a destination through the eyes of a resident can be quite different than as a tourist Try spending several weeks or more to scope out the rhythm of daily life and the accessibility of things you may take for granted. You may even want to see it at different times of the year to experience the culture, pace, and availability of creature comforts. A vacation in the vast wilderness can seem like a welcome break from your usual fast-paced lifestyle. However, will lack of accessibility to close friends, solid wi-fi or electrical grids, favourite restaurants, and well-stocked grocery stores start to weigh on you? Will large insects, or the venomous snakes and spiders seen in Central America, make you feel unsafe? What about bears or other wild predators found in North America?

While travelling in Central America, I enjoyed the simplicity, natural beauty, warmth, and friendly residents I encountered. But when I asked myself if I could live there, the answer wasn't as simple as I may have imagined. Upon returning home, I read a few blogs by Canadian and American expatriates who had made the move with an eye to the differences in lifestyle. Cultural and geographical differences provide a change of pace when you are on vacation but can feel very different when they become your everyday lifestyle. Consider whether you would be happy if these conditions were all you had access to, possibly for your entire retirement.

If you sell all your possessions and move to a country where a limited amount of money allows for a richer lifestyle, will inflation and the rising cost of housing prevent you from moving back to your native country should you regret the decision? If someone makes a bold move to a different country in an effort to relive a glorious vacation on a grander scale, they may be disappointed when it becomes their everyday reality. It is probably more advisable to move to a new location because it offers something you crave that is not available in your native country (for example, escaping Canadian winters by moving to a warmer climate). Now the question becomes: Do you move to a place like Florida and enjoy a lifestyle similar to what you're used to, or do you move to a nation that offers something completely different? Use these questions as a springboard to get you thinking about what you truly desire.

For many, staying closer to home to be near family is the most desirable choice. Many retirees have moved to a favourite vacation destination they frequented during their working lives, only to find that all their happiness came from the people in their lives rather than their location. In these cases, people often move back home to be closer to family and friends. If you choose to stay close to your hometown, consider whether a smaller relocation, like moving closer to the water or out to the country will be more conducive to the retirement of your dreams. If you want to take up sailing, maybe an oceanside retirement is just what you need. If you want a pursue a passion for gardening, maybe the country is a better match. Keep your eye on the long view. Will your retirement be more satisfying and restful if you downsize to a property that is easier to manage?

Maybe your current home suits your needs almost perfectly. If your current residence feels right, consider any relevant renovations or upgrades. Maybe you want to install a pool for swimming laps or add a patio or deck so that you can host your book club outside during the summer. Maybe you want to upgrade your kitchen and finally explore world cuisine, one country at a time. Ask yourself how your space can reflect your hobbies and passions.

WILL YOU BE RENOVATING YOUR HOME?

Life is busy, causing many of us to put off significant items on our to-do lists. If you plan to tackle home renovations or upgrades, consider doing them while you still have an active income. Renovations often don't go as planned and end up costing much more than anticipated. If that causes you to part with funds earmarked for your retirement income or to carry a large debt into retirement, it can significantly affect your retirement lifestyle. Consider the couple who plans to create a backyard oasis in which to enjoy in their newfound free time. After installing a pool, cabana, and outdoor fireplace, they may easily go over budget. Maybe they opted for a few extra bells and whistles, or maybe the price of materials went way up. It can provide a lot of peace of mind to complete and pay for these upgrades before you find yourself on a fixed income.

SHOULD YOU DOWNSIZE TO ACCESS HOME EQUITY?

If you are nearing your desired retirement age, but your portfolio has not quite made it with you, not all is lost. If your portfolio won't generate the income you need to fund your lifestyle, consider downsizing your home to access some of the equity. If you had a large family and your kids have grown and are on their own, or if you are planning to move out of the big city or relocate for other reasons, you may have a lot of wealth tied up in your home. When you sell your primary residence in Canada, you can enjoy a principal residence exemption, which means you won't pay tax on the capital gains as long as you file your tax returns correctly and have never used your home for income purposes.

A few mutual fund companies offer tax-efficient vehicles in which you can invest to create an income stream. Generally, return of capital provides the most tax-efficient form of income distribution from an investment. Simply put, if you invest a lump sum derived from the equity in your home, they will pay you out 5% income per year (some offer an 8% option as well). That income is tax-deferred (no tax slip) for the first 20 years as your original capital (adjusted cost base) is being lowered by 5% per year. When your original capital (adjusted cost base) reaches zero in the twenty-first year, future payments are taxed as a capital gain. This is a great way to defer tax to a more advantageous time in your life. The goal is to invest in a portfolio designed to create a safer return of about 6% so that when you draw out 5% income, you don't risk depleting your original investment and running out of money. It keeps producing a gain every year and that gain is the income you draw. While it will fluctuate in value over time, your capital is not at significant risk of depleting and at year-end, the amount you invested will be there to produce another year's income.

For example, let's say Linda downsizes her home to one worth $350,000 less than her original residence. After paying out the fees and expenses associated with the sale, she ends up with $300,000 (tax-free capital gain). She goes to an independent financial advisor and invests this $300,000 in an income-balanced portfolio expected to earn approximately 6% ($18,000 gain). This portfolio is held in a T-SWP (Tax-efficient Systematic Withdrawal Plan), and she starts receiving 5% ($15,000) per year or an extra $1,250 per month on top of her other sources of retirement income. The fund company does not issue a tax slip for these payments (that is how return of capital works), although Linda may pay small amounts of taxable distributions along the way. For the most part, she is maximizing cash flow and deferring tax. In the twenty-first year, her $15,000 of additional income will generate a taxable capital gain (50% of the yearly payment is now added to her income and is taxable). When Linda decides to sell her investment or dies, she will have a larger capital gain in the future (that's how deferral works). As long as you earn above the 5% distribution you are taking as income, you are not touching the principle, which will continue to earn income for you for the rest of your life.

Since a big part of your income is not taxable, you may remain in the lowest tax bracket even with your other sources of income: CPP (Canada Pension Plan), OAS (Old Age Security), Pension, RRIF (Registered Retirement Income Fund) income, etc. You may also qualify for certain benefits reserved for low-income Canadians. Finally, minimizing tax reduces the gross redemptions you need to make to fuel your lifestyle or your desired net income. This leaves more capital working for you in the markets.

If this scenario is not entirely clear, contact an independent financial advisor who represents the products of various fund companies rather than one bank or insurance company. They can explain the benefits of T-SWP in greater depth. Unfortunately, as of the writing of this book, most banks do not offer this product, but it is widely available through independent financial planners. When used correctly, it is an excellent tax deferral and a safe way to invest for income.

WILL YOU BE MAKING ANY MAJOR PURCHASES?

As we move away from the time constraints of employment or business, we find ourselves with a lot of time for the activities that bring us joy. Still, the fact is that dreams cost money and you need to make sure that you have budgeted the expense into your overall retirement plan. If you've always dreamed of a more adventurous lifestyle, consider how much of an investment is required to make this dream a reality.

For some, buying an RV (recreational vehicle) and touring across Canada or the US is a lifelong dream. Whether you choose to buy an RV new or used, they aren't cheap, and you may not have considered that, beyond the RV itself, there are many other purchases that go with the lifestyle that can quickly add up. Many RVers will talk about the benefits of having a couple of electric bikes in tow. Once you've set up camp, levelled the RV, and hooked up to electricity and water, you may need to go into town for groceries. You won't want to unhook everything just to make a small trip. In larger provincial or state parks, these bikes can also provide a great method for getting around to see the sights. Upon arrival, you may wish to ride in and see the site to make sure it suits the size and style of your recreational vehicle. In the RV world, there are endless tools and supplies to make this lifestyle smoother. Make sure to consider these when you budget.

Have you and your spouse talked about getting a couple of motorcycles? The freedom of the open road can be incredibly alluring, but like other dreams, it comes with a price tag. This should not discourage you, but it is something to think about in advance. Once you purchase your new or used bikes, get them licensed and insured, take the necessary safety courses, add a few accessories, and buy the required safety gear, you can easily spend tens of thousands of dollars. If you plan to add a trailer hitch and trailer, you are looking at an even larger investment.

For some, travel can simply be the desire to get away in a camper. For others, towing two motorcycles behind and riding specific routes on two wheels at your destination makes it a more complete and exciting adventure. BDRs (Backcountry Discovery Routes) have become popular recently in the motorcycle world. These specialized bikes are a combination of street and dirt bikes and are specially outfitted to handle the rigours of off-road routes. There are even companies who rent these bikes and guide you through an adventure over several days.

If your other hobbies, such as woodworking, photography, or diving, require specialized equipment, you need to decide whether your retirement budget will allow for these purchases or if you should acquire these things while you still have active income. Resist the urge to think that you'll never retire with all these extra expenses and instead concentrate on your priorities in the four or five years leading up to your planned retirement date. There are endless ways to trim a budget to set aside money for your big dreams.

IS IT TIME FOR A NEW CAR?

If your current vehicle is several years old or has a lot of miles on the odometer, you may decide to purchase a newer vehicle to provide peace of mind. It's safe to say that most people, given the opportunity, would rather not spend their golden years constantly repairing their cars. Next to your home, this may be your second largest purchase. Will you buy or lease a newer, low mileage vehicle or even splurge on something brand new? Do your hobbies require a different type of vehicle such as a truck? You may need one capable of towing a boat or trailer, for example. Will your household go from two vehicles down to one or vice versa? This is something worth pondering while you are still working.

DO YOU NEED TO PAY OFF YOUR MORTGAGE OR CONSUMER DEBT?

While you do not need to be debt free, your cashflow can certainly stretch further month to month if you are not carrying significant credit balances into retirement. Here are a couple of strategies to consider. If you are nearing the end of your career, you may well be in your peak earning years. This may allow you to lower the amortization and increase the principal payment on your mortgage or consumer debt to pay it off quicker. If you are six years from retirement, can you divide your outstanding balances into 72 payments and align them to be paid by your desired retirement date? You can accomplish this through additional payments to principle. Ask your mortgage provider how to do this without financial penalty.

Is it time to declutter your home from years and years of consumption? Consider selling items you don't need anymore and applying that money to your debts. Is it worth it for your household to take on a second or part-time job and use these earnings to pay off debts? If you have an extra room in your home, consider renting it to a long or short-term renter, or registering as an Airbnb host. Could you semi-retire and work seasonally or part time for the first few years of retirement to pay your debts off? Maybe you can turn one of your retirement hobbies or pastimes into additional income. Chapter 4 has more on this topic.

You may decide on a combination of these ideas or come up with some of your own for a short-term pain, long-term gain scenario. Sometimes these types of sacrifices are easier to stomach when you have that end goal in mind.

CONCLUSION

As you can see, some careful consideration in the four to five years leading up to your retirement can eliminate or significantly reduce major barriers that could prevent you from reaching your goals and fully enjoying the lifestyle you crave. I hope I've given you an idea or two that you can put into practice as you prepare for this significant life change. There is a balancing act when it comes to combining the financial aspects of being prepared for retirement with the psychological aspects of making the leap. In the next few chapters, we will cover many of the obstacles that people face psychologically and emotionally as they prepare to officially retire.

CHAPTER 2

WHAT IS YOUR RETIREMENT PERSONALITY?

THERE HAVE BEEN several publications that discuss retirement personalities. Some are written from the purely psychological perspective while others speak more to the main activity that describes a person's lifestyle. Since this guide is aimed at getting you to think about how to create the ultimate retirement, this chapter will be a combination of these two approaches. I have identified nine different retirement personalities, although some people will be a combination of two or more. Some people may identify with differing personalities. It is also the case that people may move between these personalities at different phases of retirement.

THE LEISURE SEEKER

North Americans are known for living fast-paced lives with little vacation time. As we shed the shackles of employment or business and long for simpler lives, the Leisure Seeker is someone who just needs to slow down. If you had a particularly stressful job, were a single parent, worked more than one job, or needed to commute to work daily, leisure may be the first order of business for you. The Leisure Seeker may particularly enjoy getting out of bed whenever they want and not having too many commitments during the week. Letting each day unfold without a solid plan may give them much-needed relief from the structure and commitment they were accustomed to during their working lives. They often enjoy spending time with their children or grandchildren, sipping coffee on the deck, lunches with friends, and the odd getaway. You can often see a little spring in their step and a smile on their face as they enjoy life on their own terms. Catching up on projects cast aside during their busier work lives can provide a sense of achievement.

These people can find pleasure in just about anything so long as it doesn't tie them down. There is probably a little Leisure Seeker in most retirees, but for some, this personality type describes one of their main retirement lifestyle goals. For others, this is the first of many phases they go through, as described in Chapter 5.

THE WORKAHOLIC

As I've met with financial planning clients over the past 26 years, there have always been the group that say, "I'll never retire." These people often prefer to be on the move and derive great satisfaction from their careers. When I talk more with these clients, the conversation often reveals that they have never put much thought into creating a plan for retirement. Quite frankly, that's one of the many reasons I felt that people could benefit from a book like this one. If they are forced into retirement unwillingly, the Workaholic may take on consulting work or some other version of self-employment related to their former occupation. They sometimes decide that retirement is a good time to pursue the business they have always dreamed of starting. Some entrench themselves in volunteer work and do a lot of good for their communities.

There is an African proverb that speaks to this retirement personality. I do not know the original author, but it goes like this. Every morning in Africa, a gazelle wakes up. It knows it must outrun the fastest lion or it will be killed. Every morning, a lion wakes up. It knows it must outrun the slowest gazelle or it will starve to death. It doesn't matter whether you are a lion or gazelle, when the sun comes up, you had better start running.

THE RECLUSE

Unlike the Leisure Seeker, the Recluse tends to disengage from life. This is possibly the only negative retirement personality. Sometimes, these people were forced into retirement against their wishes and don't know how to occupy their time. There are sometimes other good reasons such as a failed marriage or past trauma that cause these folks to avoid other people at all costs. Upon retirement, some people need time to formulate a plan or figure out their next move and, unfortunately, those plans never come to fruition. If you feel you can identify with this lifestyle and its problematic for you, you may consider reaching out to family or friends or even a counsellor for some guidance.

With that being said, there are folks who have always dreamed of the cabin in the wilderness for their retirement. Many introverts quite enjoy their own time and solitude. There are even shows on

TV about mountain men and women who like to remove themselves from society and fly into town once a month for necessary supplies. I am sure there are more than a couple of people who could do this for a month or even a summer, or it could be a phase that they use to decompress after a life of punching the clock.

THE ADVENTURER

Near the other end of the spectrum is the Adventurer. People with this personality type don't view retirement as an end but rather a new beginning. This is what I mean when I say that you shouldn't simply retire from something but retire to something. Sometimes, Adventurers are making up for lost time or hope to do the things they put off because of life obligations. In some cases, adventure and excitement are what drives them. While it can be difficult to get up at 7:00 a.m. to go to work, it is often easier to get up at 6:30 a.m. for a day of fun. The adventure lifestyle can define a person's retirement for as long as they are physically able. There are often hints of the other personalities in their everyday lives, but everything is an experience.

While not a full-fledged Jet Setter, Adventurers love the opportunity to take extended vacations rather than continuing to take the rushed one to two weeks away that they had while working. While travelling, some people wish they had an extra week to visit a nearby town or city. They dream of the day they can extend their trips. For the Adventurer, travel is not simply a holiday at a resort. They want to immerse themselves in the culture of their destination and take in as many things as they can. This can lead to a fast-paced lifestyle that may seem exhausting to the Leisure Seeker. Adventurers are not usually defined by one main activity but rather by their desire to create many different experiences on an ongoing basis. The aphorism that comes to mind here is, "It's not how many breaths you take, but the moments that take your breath away."

For the Adventurer, a list of the daily activities they plan to do during retirement will likely fill more than a single page. For these folks, the pre-retirement phase may be integral in preparing them to hit the ground running. Some Adventurers may decide to buy a piece of land and build a home to start their new chapter. Others may acquire all the equipment for their exciting new hobbies or sell everything and convert an old school bus into a camper so they can travel across the country. Some may think that these are great ideas but wonder how people can afford to pursue these dreams. Often, it requires a major change such as selling the family home and many possessions even several times, to get to the next adventure. For many people that is too uncomfortable. Many people have had the "if I won the lottery" conversation or dream, but finding the energy and passion has fizzled out by the time they were financially able to retire. During client meetings over the years, I have witnessed that the true Adventurer is methodically planning details well in advance and can't wait until the day they can put all their plans into motion.

THE ARTIST OR CREATOR

For the creative soul, retirement encompasses a new lifestyle. This can include musicians, visual artists, painters, sculptors, and even wood and metal workers. Chefs may also identify with this personality. These folks are driven by passion. Retirement can be a time when they immerse themselves in their craft. The Artist may open a gallery or sell their pieces online or at shows throughout the year. They may open a custom motorcycle shop where they build and showcase bikes. For the musician, playing in a band, recording music, and going on tour may be things to which they devote endless hours. This can be an excellent way to supplement retirement income, as outlined in Chapter 4.

For the Artist, travel may be more culturally driven, featuring trips to find inspiration by exploring galleries, museums, and beautiful historical sites. The creative soul often enjoys the company of others where they can meet to discuss ideas. Hosting dinner or cocktail parties with other creative personalities is definitely in their wheelhouse. Some people use retirement to join a local theatre group, dabble in acting, and attend performances on the weekends. The Artist may gravitate to communities that celebrate the arts. Retirement could be the time that they finally sit down and write the book they have always wanted to write. The newfound freedom of retirement serves to release the pent-up creativity that often got stifled by the demands of their busy lifestyles. Some of their best creative work may come out in their retirement years. Like they say, it's never too late.

THE SEARCHER

When I think of the Searcher, I think of the high school student who hasn't quite decided what they want to do with their life yet. The Searcher will often try several different avenues before they discover what they like to do best. Rather than following a definitive plan, they tend to uncover things by trial and error. Retirement can be thought of as one of the career paths we follow in our lifetimes. But rather than getting paid a formalized wage, we get paid in experiences.

If you identify with the Searcher, I hope this book will help you find what you love to do with your free time. You may also benefit from working with a counsellor who has an affinity for helping people find direction in life. For some, the process of trial and error is a fun journey within itself. Often, when children are younger, they jump from one sport or activity to another. They may not become the best at their current activity, but they can become a very well-rounded individual as a result. Adults can essentially go through the same process. Don't see it as a negative that you haven't settled into one avocation. Just enjoy the journey on your own time.

THE JET SETTER

When I was much younger, travel wasn't as common as it is these days, and we certainly didn't see as many people travelling to far-away or exotic locations. I am sure the internet has played a role in making the world seem smaller and more accessible. Social media has given a lot of people FOMO (fear of missing out). Sometimes when we see others doing things we haven't, we feel the need to do the same. This has been called the bandwagon effect or herd mentality. Regardless of their reasons, people are travelling farther and more often these days. For some, jet-setting can be a euphoric phase in the first stage of retirement. For others, it can last for years or even decades. The internet has made planning a trip something nearly anyone can do. Some Jet Setters have extensive bucket lists of places they want to see.

One time, my daughter and I were driving when Darius Rucker's song, "For the First Time", came on the radio. She thought that the lyric, "when was the last time you did something for the first time," was a bit odd. I went on to explain that there was a first time she rode a bike. I remembered her first soccer game and so on. I told her that when you reach my age there are fewer and fewer firsts as we have already had the opportunity to explore so many things.

Travel, however, is one way people my age can continually try new things. This can be one of the elements that keeps the Jet Setter so engaged. For some people, it's one or two trips per year, every year. The rest of the time they are dreaming, exploring, and planning their next trip. The extreme Jet Setter may travel extensively or even continuously for years. There are people who retire, sell all their worldly possessions, and trade them for this lifestyle. Some retirees work at a part-time job strictly to save travel money. You may be fortunate enough to have saved for a decent retirement, but if travel is a luxury outside of your budget, Chapter 4 may give you some great ideas on how to turn a hobby or interest into a supplementary source of income to see all those places you have dreamed of.

THE ATHLETE

This is a retirement personality where proper health and nutrition plays a vital role. The healthy retiree may identify with the Athlete personality. These people are always active. You see them signing up for races and even marathons. They may spend a lot of time cycling and plan extended cycling trips where they intend to see the destination on two wheels. There are travel services that cater to cyclists, offering package deals for flights, hotels, bike rentals, and tour guides. For some, yoga is a favourite activity, and they may become certified to teach classes from home or at an outdoor studio. Scuba divers and wind surfers could also fall into this category. Some people meet a group weekly to participate in their favourite sport and love the camaraderie. Some Athletes spend much of their time skiing the slopes or hiking any trail they can find. The common theme is that they lead an active lifestyle predominantly devoted to one or more sports or other activities.

If they aren't as active as they used to be, they may become a coach. Some hold fitness classes in things like martial arts and pass on their years of knowledge to the next generation. This is another area where a person can generate some additional retirement income. If you are younger and an avid sports nut, this may persuade you to stay in top shape until your retirement plan frees up more time for you to enjoy these activities.

THE SCHOLAR

There are people among us that have an endless thirst for knowledge. They feel alive when they are learning new things. Not everyone gets an education simply to land a job. For some, education is essential because it allows them to see the world with an open mind, engage in more stimulating conversations, and understand and appreciate more of the world around them. There are retirees whose favourite place is in the library amid the glorification of humanity.

The Scholar's dream vacation could be to visit a centuries-old library in a favourite European city. They may attend classes at the local college or university or become a member of a society devoted to exploring a topic such as astronomy, history, or even dinosaurs. The topics you can study are limitless, and as the old expression goes, the more you learn, the less you know. Some Scholars pride themselves on the extensive libraries they have built in their homes where they can curl up in a favourite chair and scour through their well-loved books. Some people study ancient civilizations or religions and devote years to thoroughly understanding them. They may host workshops and talks to further educate their peers. For others, a great day involves visiting a quaint bookstore in a small town and making some new acquisitions.

SUMMARY

There are endless ways to spend your days, weeks, and years during retirement. I hope this chapter sets your creativity in motion and helps you identify your retirement personalities. If reading one of the descriptions above makes you feel alive, consider how you can use your newfound freedom to explore and enjoy these archetypes. Not everyone will align strictly with only one personality at a time or during the entirety of their retirement years. Life can throw curve balls your way and things such as health or finances can sometimes dictate your choices. Try to make gratitude a part of your daily routine if you are lucky enough to retire young and healthy enough to create a glorious retirement. That truly is a wonderful gift!

Now let's move on and delve deeper into the specific activities with which you may choose to occupy your days and weeks.

CHAPTER 3

WHAT DO YOU DO
WITH YOUR TIME?

ONE OF THE number one things new retirees are asked by colleagues and friends is, "What do you do with your time?" Unfortunately, we have been programmed to get up and go to school or work for most of our lives. We are used to structure and discipline, but what we are not taught is how to structure our days once we become fully retired and don't need to work anymore.

As I have mentioned a few times throughout this book, the successful retiree doesn't just from retire from something but rather to something. Getting up early to work at a stressful job so that we can pay our bills can be very taxing. However, it can be far easier to get up early for a great vacation or an exciting day with family and friends. The goal is to create a life that we can't wait to wake up to and experience.

The possibilities are endless, but for those who are struggling to come up with ideas, I have assembled a handy list. This list is not exhaustive by any means. It is designed to get your creative juices flowing. Many of the ideas can be incorporated into travel destinations and many can turn into additional sources of income. When it comes to travel, some people plan a trip and just go while others select destinations that dovetail with their favourite activity. Examples of these might be wine tasting in parts of France or Italy or skiing in Colorado.

With each item on the list, I have noted which ones are common during travel or can be used to generate income: for example, *wine tasting (travel)* or *woodworking (income).* The next chapter explores how retirees have turned their hobbies into sources of income in greater depth. Some of these ideas can turn into full-fledged avocations while others are things you may wish to incorporate into your life purely out of interest or well-being. Let's take a look!

THINGS TO DO WHEN YOU RETIRE

1. **Adopt a pet.** It's no secret that pets are great companions, offering faithful and unconditional love to their humans. But did you know they can also help reduce stress, improve mood, and lower your blood pressure? There are many animals in need of a loving home in Canada. In 2018, for example, 81,000 cats and 30,000 dogs were taken into shelters. Ask shelter staff for guidance as you consider which pet may be right for you.

2. **Learn an instrument (income).** Performing music is for the brain what circuit training is for the body. Playing a musical instrument engages almost every part of the brain at once. The process of practising music strengthens brain functions and keeps you sharp. You may want to dust off a musical instrument you or

your children once played. Pursuing music can provide the opportunity to play with other musicians or just play for your family and friends. If you focus and excel at an instrument, you could join a band or work part time as a musician. This can lead to some extra retirement income.

3. **Become a gardener or garden expert (income).** Growing a garden can provide many benefits. It is a chance to get outdoors, exercise, enjoy the fresh air and sunshine, and grow some healthy vegetables. Have you developed a wealth of gardening knowledge over the years? Your experience will be welcomed by novices wanting to create a serene space in their yards. Consider offering your services. You can start by posting an ad on a community Facebook page. Then, your consultation service could be a walk-through of the client's garden to offer guidance and answer questions. There are often community clubs and information sessions which you could attend or even host. Hosting these events has the added benefit of providing the social time that many retirees desire.

4. **Become a photographer (travel, income).** Photography is an excellent hobby because it gives you an excuse to explore new places (if you need one). You can join photography clubs and meet other hobbyists. Look for courses through local photography stores or your community centre. Photography can be dovetailed with your travels and even offers many ways to supplement your retirement income. I cover many of these ways in the next chapter, so keep reading!

5. **Become a tour guide (travel, income).** Do you live in a tourist area? Maybe there is a museum in town. Becoming a tour guide is a great way to share your knowledge and passion with others. Some people make a living hosting tours, whether it be in their hometown or in their favourite vacation spot. You can even combine

this with a love of cycling, motorcycles, Segway, Jeeps, or other means of transportation.

6. Snowshoeing and downhill or cross-country skiing (travel, income). Most of Canada experiences long, snowy winters. Taking up a winter activity is a great way to stay active and continue to get fresh air. Snowshoeing and downhill or cross-country skiing are activities that can be modified to suit different ability levels. Start by renting equipment. You can also often find used items. There are so many beautiful destinations where skiing is a common activity and becoming a ski instructor can be a fun way to supplement your retirement income while sharing your love of the sport with newcomers.

7. Develop your cooking skills (income). Mealtimes can feel rushed during our working years. However, retirement may be a chance to develop your cooking skills. You can find classes through community colleges, your municipality, or private schools. Or just watch cooking shows and videos to try out different recipes. This is another area that can lead to a source of income. Many retirees sell their baked goods or other creations at trade shows, markets, farm stands, etc. Some people sell foods from their native country out of their homes (for example, perogies and cabbage rolls for those with Ukrainian heritage).

8. Explore countries by rail (travel). There are so many interesting places to see and explore in Canada. Remember, the journey is as important as the destination! Travelling by rail can be a low-stress and fun option, and Via Rail offers discounts if you're over 60. Many countries offer famous picturesque train trips. For example, there's the Bernina Express in the Swiss Alps. Travel can be more than just seeing a destination. By adding a little creativity, your trips can come alive into full-fledged adventures.

9. **Fishing.** Fishing is a sport beloved by many worldwide. Whether you live near a body of water, have a boat, or fish from shore, you can enjoy countless hours with this activity. A little online research about equipment and technique is all you need to get started, but you could also attend fishing shows in your area. If you don't live near a lake or river, renting a cottage or camping may help you explore new areas through the lens of your love of fishing.

10. **Golfing (travel).** Golf is often associated with retirement and carries many benefits, first and foremost the way it promotes fitness through walking. Golfing also promotes social activity. You can enter the golf course as a foursome, but people who go alone are often put into a group of four as well, giving them the chance to meet new people who share their interest. If you are a passionate golfer, this hobby can also lead to vacationing to places where you can play courses of all different levels.

11. **Focus on healthy eating.** With more time for yourself, you can finally make healthy eating a priority. Focus on finding sustainable, healthy cuisines that suit your lifestyle and include foods that you enjoy. If you need help, try to access dietitian services through a local seniors' centre. If you know a lot about healthy eating already, you could even support other retirees by offering this service yourself. While this hobby may not fill your timetable, it is another important element to staying healthy and fit. No one wants to plan a glorious retirement only to be not well enough to enjoy it!

12. **Get a personal trainer or join a group fitness class.** As with healthy eating, retirement offers a chance to refocus on physical fitness. A lack of time is always an easy excuse not to exercise, but now you have the time. A personal trainer can help create a plan for you. Or you could join a group fitness class. Check with

your doctor before taking on a new fitness regime. Exercise can play a crucial part in keeping you healthy enough to enjoy all the activities discussed in this chapter.

13. Get involved in local politics. If politics interest you, consider getting involved locally. You could run for councillor or lend your support to someone else's campaign. You could also join a municipal committee. Some municipalities may have committees on topics you are passionate about, like education and environmental issues. It is a great way to keep you busy and involved.

14. Get to know your neighbours. Do you know your neighbours? Now that you're not running out to work every day, perhaps you can get to know the people who live around you. Maybe there's another retired person nearby who would join you for daily walks or any of the activities listed in this chapter.

15. Go back to school. Many retirees take courses during retirement, and some have even completed graduate degrees! If you enjoy learning, retirement may be a great time to dive back in. You could take formal courses through a college or university or try an online learning platform. You could also investigate learning options through your public library or local college. For the Scholar, the possibilities and topics really are endless. You know the old saying, "The more you learn, the less you know."

16. Go geocaching. Geocaching is like a worldwide treasure hunt. To play, you download a free app and use GPS coordinates to find hidden geocaches. There are millions around the world, and probably some very close to you. Once you gain experience, you can even hide your own geocache for others to find! Geocaching can help you explore new places at home or while travelling. It could also be a fun activity to do with grandchildren.

17. **Go to festivals.** Festivals are a great excuse to visit a new town or city. Whether you enjoy music of any kind, cars, art, fishing, fitness, crafting, or food, you can find a festival that will appeal to your interests!

18. **Join a choir.** Many people join choirs in retirement. Doing so gives you the opportunity to meet new people and perform for others. Some choirs even enter competitions. To find a choir in your area, try a quick Google search, ask friends, or inquire at your library or a local music store.

19. **Join a group for retirees.** There are many social groups for retirees. Many seniors' centres and social media platforms list such groups. It can be a great way to meet people with common interests to you.

20. **Join a non-profit board or committee.** Non-profit organizations often look for people to share their skills, knowledge, and experience on boards or other volunteer committees. If committee work appeals to you, look for a non-profit whose mission you want to support while giving back to your community.

21. **Join or create a travel group (travel).** Travelling with other people can be a lot of fun! It's also a great way to organize and save on excursions you may not otherwise be able to do. Ask around to see if there's a travel group you can join. You can often find such groups on social media. If you don't find an existing group to join, consider teaming up with some friends to create one! You can work with a travel agent or, if you're keen, do your own booking. Of course, always use caution and common sense when agreeing to travel with new people.

22. **Learn a language.** There are many reasons to learn a new language. Perhaps you want to be able to communicate with locals

while travelling, maybe you like the brain-building benefits of language learning, or maybe you've just always wanted to speak multiple languages. Retirement is a great time to act if this is a bucket-list goal for you. Look for courses in your community or try an online program like Duolingo.

23. **Try stand-up paddleboarding, canoeing, or kayaking (travel).** Stand-up paddleboarding involves standing on a large board and using a long paddle to manoeuvrer yourself through the water. It requires balance, but it's an activity that most people can do with some guidance. If you live near water, find out if there's a place nearby to rent a paddleboard. Often you can join a group class too. Canoeing and kayaking are also great ways to explore waterways in your area or while travelling. All of these activities add fitness to your life and contribute to positive mental health through sunshine, fresh air, and peaceful, low-intensity exertion.

24. **Learn to paint, draw, or discover the visual arts (income).** Creating art can help to reduce stress and boost self-esteem. Learning to paint or taking up painting again can provide a great creative outlet in retirement. It can also lead to a greater appreciation for the work you see in art galleries while travelling. Plus, if you find a distinct art style of your own, you can gain extra income by selling your work online or at creative markets.

25. **Learn woodworking (income).** There's a special kind of satisfaction that comes from constructing something from wood. Even if you've never used a power tool before, you can learn woodworking if the idea interests you. Check the continuing education catalogue of a local community college for courses. Many retirees have turned their passion for woodworking into a source of income through selling their creations.

26. **Map your family history.** It's never been easier to uncover your family history. If you haven't created your family tree, retirement is a great time to take on the project. You could even team up with a sibling or other family member and work on it together. There are several websites, like Ancestry and 23andMe, that can help you get started. You can also check with your library for resources and support.

27. **Mentor others.** You have skills and experience to share with the world. If you like coaching and mentoring others, find out if there are opportunities to share your expertise at your previous workplace or through your local community centre. You could also volunteer through a local organization like Big Brothers Big Sisters, which has been proven to make a real difference in children's lives.

28. **Consider an e-commerce business (income).** If you make or collect items that others may want to purchase, you can make some extra money by opening an Etsy or Shopify store. There are some excellent how-to videos on YouTube to get you started and teach you the finer details of running an online business.

29. **Practise meditation or yoga (income).** Meditation is one of those beneficial things that may seem tough to fit into life, but in retirement, you may find it easier to set aside 10 to 30 minutes a day for a meditation practice. There are many apps available to help, such as Headspace, Calm, or Insight Timer. Yoga is a complementary practice, combining elements of mediation, stretching, and strength training to promote mental and physical health. Enrolling in yoga classes can be a great way to interact with people who share a common interest, and many people go on to become certified yoga instructors and run classes in their area.

30. **Start a blog (travel, income).** A blog is a great way to document your ideas and experiences while building your writing and technical skills. For example, you could blog about a specific topic you're interested in or create a lifestyle blog covering various elements of day-to-day life. There is also the potential to turn this into an income source and combine it with travel. Some people's greatest dream is to visit their favourite places and write about their travels on their blog.

31. **Start a business (income).** We've already covered a few business ideas, like becoming a garden consultant and opening an Etsy shop. If you have an idea or skill set that others value, consider running a small business that plays to these strengths!

32. **RVing (travel).** RVing is a very popular way to cruise the nation and enjoy your favourite destinations. It also can be a more cost-effective way to see many places. The US has embraced RVing offering many locations and facilities for the enthusiast to enjoy along the way. You may be surprised about the number of places you can stay. This hobby can become an active lifestyle that provides years of enjoyment. Some people take it to the next level and convert an old school bus into a home that they park in new locations on a regular basis. Go online and check out the school bus conversions others have done. There are some amazing transformations!

33. **Take up cycling (travel).** Cycling is a great way to explore different areas. But if the idea of cycling on a road intimidates you, don't fret. Instead, look up hybrid bikes—these are a cross between a road bike and a mountain bike. They have slightly thicker tires and a more upright seated position, and they're perfect for exploring the many rail trails (flat stretches of trail where railways used to be) around Canada. Many people choose to see their favourite destinations on two wheels.

34. **Learn to ride a motorcycle (travel).** People who ride motorcycles tend to be part of a subculture or community. They often meet in groups to ride their favourite locations, whether those destinations are at home or abroad. Many countries offer destination vacations in the form of motorcycle tours. Couples often see motorcycling as a way to connect and enjoy an activity together. You can begin by getting licensed, then taking a safety class. Then decide whether you want to ride dirt, street, or even explore BDRs. In the last few years, Backcountry Discovery Routes have become a huge new category in the motorcycle world.

35. **Volunteer.** Probably not surprisingly, in Canada, older adults are more likely than other age groups to be top volunteers, meaning they spend the most time per year volunteering. Volunteering can help provide a sense of purpose and is a great way to meet new people. It also enables you to share your unique gifts, skills, and knowledge. It's good for you and others!

36. **Work part time (income).** Where have you always wanted to work? Retirement is a chance to try a part-time job that aligns with your interests. Are you a coffee aficionado? Try working as a barista! Love cars? Why not work as a courtesy driver for a dealership? You could work at a golf course or teaching sewing classes. The possibilities are endless, and you may welcome the interaction, chance to use your skills, and extra pocket money!

37. **Write a book (income).** The saying goes that everyone has a novel in them. Perhaps you have a skill, story, or passion you would love to share with others. This can be an engrossing creative activity, and services like Kindle Direct Publishing and Ingram Spark make publishing a book yourself easier than you may have thought.

38. **Diving (travel).** While you may not be a certified diver yet, it is never too late to try. You can begin by searching local diving shops to see who offers certification courses. Once certified, you can spend countless hours exploring bodies of water both locally and abroad. It is another activity that can take you to places you never thought you would go.

BECOMING A SUCCESSFUL RETIREE

"Successful retiree" may sound like an odd thing to say. However, some of most satisfied retirees that I have come across have added a level of excitement and creativity to their daily lives as well as their adventures and travel. Travel doesn't always have to involve flights and faraway places. Sometimes travel means visiting a neighbouring town or going to see a friend or family member who lives relatively close to you. I'll share a few examples.

For some, travel involves going to an all-inclusive for a week. These holidays can be incredibly relaxing and enjoyable. For the Leisure Seeker, this may be just what the doctor ordered as they attempt to unwind from years of punching a clock and living a fast-paced lifestyle. The Artist might see things differently. For them, going to Europe to visit some of the most unique galleries in old towns may add a layer of excitement that speaks to their passion.

Some individuals and couples seek more adventure. They may decide to buy a pair of ATVs (all-terrain vehicles) and tour ATV parks across Canada or the US. This can become a lifestyle where they acquire and customize their ATVs and go to shows in the spring featuring the latest equipment. A camper may become part of their lifestyle, so they always have a place to stay on their travels. This is a natural environment in which to meet people with similar interests, and these retirees often love the thrill and excitement of exploring new routes in unfamiliar places. Not every retiree is independently wealthy. A hobby like this can be enjoyed on a tighter budget by buying a good quality used machine, adding a trailer hitch to their present vehicle, and getting some decent safety equipment all for under $10,000. Choosing accommodations that are budget friendly all make this a reality for the retiree on a budget.

If you are more of an Athlete personality or enjoy golfing during retirement, maybe your big expense is playing a round or two at a dream course once per year. You can make golf part of your travel destinations and play many different courses over a period of many years.

For the wine enthusiast, you may discover that the local college or local wine store offers wine pairing nights where you learn to cook a meal and pair it with the perfect glass. You may start a wine club with other enthusiasts where you meet once per week to give a presentation and enjoy a glass with some favourite cheeses. Once a year, you and your club could travel to a place like Napa Valley in California to enjoy a few cabernets. Working part time at a winery could supplement your retirement income while doing something you enjoy. Engaging in part-time work when you don't need the money to survive can be enjoyable. Some may go so far as to create a tasting room in their basement or garage. It can add a fun element to these get togethers.

Using a hobby or interest as a springboard for social activity, incorporating it into travel, and even attending shows or festivals can turn the hobby into more of a lifestyle. If you don't currently have a hobby or interest you enjoy, you may identify with the Searcher personality covered in Chapter 2. You may find yourself trying several things before you settle on one or two things that you are passionate about. And that is a great way to keep things new and exciting.

HOW TO PLAN YOUR WEEK?

A tool I have found helpful when discussing retirement with clients who are a few years away is to create a chart like the one below and try to fill in activities from Monday to Friday, morning, afternoon, and evening. Most of us have been occupying our weekends and days off our entire lives. However, many people have a tough time replacing the time they devoted to commuting to their jobs, working, and commuting home. It is likely that their occupation or business has been the single biggest consumer of time for most of their lives. And for many, it represents an emotional challenge to complete this exercise. Even the person who enjoys many hobbies and interests can find this to be a valuable exercise when it comes to planning their retirement. Having some structure in your timetable can help you deal with the losses that can occur during retirement.

Monday	Tuesday	Wednesday	Thursday	Friday
Morning	Morning	Morning	Morning	Morning
Afternoon	Afternoon	Afternoon	Afternoon	Afternoon
Night	Night	Night	Night	Night

HOW TO PLAN A TRIP

Some people find comfort in familiarity and have no plans to venture much farther than their hometown, and that's perfectly fine. Others have big travel plans. If a constrained budget, family obligations, or a lack of vacation time has prevented you from travelling much in the past, you may find the following information especially useful as you take advantage of your newfound freedom by travelling to your bucket-list destinations.

Over the years, I have had many people comment on my ability to plan a trip that goes smoothly every time. I will share my process in the hopes that you pick up a few good ideas. This process is especially helpful if you plan to visit several cities over a shorter period of two weeks or so.

SITE-SEEING TRIPS

When planning a trip, I find it helpful to draw a line across a piece of paper, then plot the dates I plan be away. This serves as a helpful timeline when I'm selecting flights, hotels, and pretty much anything else I need to organize. It helps to visualize the timeline. From there, I book the flights first so that I make sure they are available. Flight times could determine when and where you need to book hotels or other elements of your trip. There are many sites offering discount flights these days, so it may be worth it to quickly check two or three to make sure you're paying the best fare.

Next, I determine which cities I will be staying in on which dates. This is especially important if you are planning to visit several cities over your vacation adventure. I tend to have two browsers open during this stage. While comparing hotels, I use Google Maps to search their distance from the airport. I may want to fly into a city and then walk or take a short cab ride to where I am staying. This helps me narrow down my choices. If I am departing by train a couple of days later, I may stay in a different hotel on the last night in that city so that I can walk to the train station on the day of my departure. The same applies if you are using a bus or boat to get to your next city.

You can usually see modes of transportation online while you are planning and decide upon the best way to get around. When booking hotels, you may choose to use the same chain or travel site, earning points for each stay. This can sometimes result in one or two free hotel stays throughout your trip. At the very least, you may get a discount stay along the way by cashing in your points.

Let's say I want to pick five cities in Italy to sample over two weeks. I may use an app like Visit A City to determine how long I need to spend in each city to see the major sites I want to see. Apps like this often let you add and subtract major tourist sites and map out a linear route to see them all over the course of a day, moving from one end of the city to the other. They will also show you the average time it takes to complete your route. You can click on each site and see a description along with any entry fees. It may be wise to start your tour at the farthest site from your hotel and work your way back to your home base. When you are tired out from your day, you won't have to make your way across town to get back to your shower or bed.

Planning like this also allows you to see how much time you have left over for lounging by the pool, enjoying dinner, or sharing drinks on the town. If you don't do any research on what you hope to see, you may find yourself wandering aimlessly, trying to figure out where to go.

Lastly, I have found that researching the places you hope to see in advance creates a wonderful sense of anticipation. When you finally get there, it is exhilarating to experience the sights you have been reading about for weeks.

It is important to look at a map online and decide upon the order you plan to visit these five cities, so you are not travelling back and forth, wasting time and money. Lastly, depending on how much ground you plan to cover, you may fly into one city and back home out of another. Otherwise, you could have a very lengthy journey back to the original airport.

Once you've planned these cities out and selected hotels, you can see your trip on the timeline you drew. Some people might think this sounds rigid or lacking in spontaneity. But you can literally do anything you want and adjust and adapt when you get there. At least, you have places booked to stay and won't find yourself wasting time searching for hotels at the end of a day. Secondly, the process outlined above may be a lot easier than you think.

Tours to special destinations can and will book up quickly, but since your journey is already laid out, you can see if you want to add one or more tours to your trip well in advance, avoiding the disappointment of discovering a tour is full when you arrive. Sites like Viator offer a variety of tours at different price points, so it can be as elaborate or simple as you want. The Viator office has always been there for me when I arrive for my tour. No one wants to prepay for a tour only to arrive at an empty building. Whichever site you choose, read a few online reviews to see if previous users were happy.

If you plan carefully, you can avoid the need to rent a car. If your trip requires one, you can usually find a rental when you arrive. However, booking one in advance may save you time and headaches. Just make sure that you can easily get to the car rental venue from the airport. Some are offsite several kilometres away.

This process can prove useful for the traveller who feels safer knowing that the logistics of their trip are booked. Some travellers prefer the idea of landing in a new place with a backpack and no itinerary. They like to immerse themselves in the culture and see what the day brings them. For others, the thought of that is very unsettling. Your retirement; your choice!

RELAXING TRIPS:

If adventures like the one above aren't your cup of tea and you dream of just lying in the sun at a tropical resort, there are still a couple of things to consider. Let's say you want to plan a week at a Caribbean resort. Find a site you are comfortable using (Expedia and TripAdvisor are tried and true options) and enter your search criteria. When you find a couple of resorts that you would like to compare, use a site like Trip Advisor to read reviews. Some people like to complain, so take reviews with a grain of salt. Still, if you see the same comment appearing over and over, it is likely based on truth.

When it comes to all-inclusive packages, I like to check how many a la carte restaurants there are to choose from. Eating the same thing every night for a week can get boring. Check what the dress code is for dinners and look at the number of rooms or size of the resort to determine how much walking you are likely to be doing. This will give you some guidance on how to pack for your stay. You may also wish to see how close the resort is to the airport. After a long travel day (driving to the airport, shuttling to your gate, sitting for hours on a plane, etc.), you may not want to spend two more hours on the shuttle as it drops people off to their resorts.

If you are leaving a wintery climate to go somewhere warm, consider packing shorts and a t-shirt in your carry-on (and don't forget flip-flops). When you arrive at a climate 25 degrees warmer than where you left, you will be glad to rid yourself of your winter coat and boots. Packing a couple of snacks (check airline restrictions for this) may help get you through the flight. If you tend to sleep on planes, consider packing a toothbrush and travel-sized toothpaste so you can freshen up when you wake up. Finally, it is always a good idea to download a game or two or bring a book or magazine to help you pass the time on your flight.

In the month or so leading up to your trip, prices for the same package can vary. Checking daily can be beneficial if it doesn't make you too anxious. Book when you see the price drop. I have saved hundreds, even thousands, over the years by doing this. This information may seem obvious to the seasoned traveller. But if you haven't had much travel experience before, I hope you have gained a good idea or two.

EXTENDED TRIPS:

If you are planning an extended trip like heading south for a month or more during the winter, your location will play a big role in your enjoyment. If you are visiting a place you have gone to in the past, you may find it relatively easy to select your location. If you plan to stay in one area, you can phone resorts to see how much they charge for an extended stay. You may be able to negotiate discounts for not using selected services like daily housekeeping, for example. Conversely, you may decide that an Airbnb or VRBO (online marketplace for vacation rentals) is a better choice for longer stays. Places with kitchens and laundry can help save you money by not having to dine in restaurants every day and sending your laundry out.

If you haven't been to an area before, you can weigh the benefits of booking a hotel for a few nights until you know where you want to settle in. Of course, in this case, there is a risk that choices may be limited if you wait until you arrive. Extended trips can take on as many different nuances as there are people, so with time, you will learn what details are important to you and which are not. You will learn tips and tricks to make your travels easier and more enjoyable.

Common sense and caution can go a long way when travelling. At your destination, you may run into someone who seems very friendly and asks lots of questions. Though this person may be genuine, you are often better served by keeping your answers vague. If someone asks about your itinerary and you say that you are leaving the next day, they know the chances of you changing your trip to call the police and recover a stolen item are reduced. Instead, say you haven't decided yet. Do not share the specifics of where you are staying. By disclosing your location, you increase the risk of someone breaking in during the night and suffering an assault or worse. When asked where you are staying, it is safer to respond with something general like, "An Airbnb in the city." If they keep pursuing an answer, it may be a greater indication that they are up to no good.

Wearing name brand fashion and jewellery can make you stand out as a potential candidate for theft. Many destinations experience theft or violent crime. Even if your destination is not cited as a high crime area, you can take steps to reduce risks. Never set your electronics down or leave your valuables unattended. Many thieves are experts at targeting unsuspecting tourists who are distracted and having a good time. It goes without saying that caution needs to be exercised when accepting a drink or ride with a stranger. This information is by no means designed to discourage travel. Your travels can simply be much safer when you follow a few safety rules and use common sense.

Again, the seasoned traveller may find a lot of this obvious. However, I have come across enough people who have asked how I plan these adventures that I felt these precautions were worth including in this guide.

In the next chapter, we discuss how to turn one of your hobbies into an additional source of income. If you and your financial planner have determined that you will have a decent amount of income to pay all your day-to-day living expenses but not a lot of extra for travel or adventure, you may consider ways to fund your travel account. A part-time job or small business, whether a couple of days per week or seasonal, can allow you to save $5,000–$10,000 per year that you can earmark for travel and adventure.

CHAPTER 4

TURNING A HOBBY INTO ADDITIONAL RETIREMENT INCOME

MOST RETIREES WHO have worked with an independent financial planner throughout their careers have accumulated a decent financial nest egg. Some employers offer pension plans or group RRSPs (Register Retirement Savings Plans). An individual may have seven or more careers over the course of their lifetime, resulting in vastly different amounts saved through these group savings plans. The big question is always how much do you need to retire on? The answer lies in lifestyle.

A typical retiree who goes into retirement after paying off their mortgage and consumer debt will still have some fixed costs. They will likely have to account for expenses like property tax, gas, hydro electricity, car and house insurance, and telecommunications like phone, internet, and TV subscriptions. As of 2023, these expenses will probably come to $1,300–$1,500 per month. You can easily add these costs up for your present situation. The income you need above your fixed costs is where lifestyle comes in.

Variable costs such as groceries, car payments, rent, travel, and personal care, as well as funding one's hobbies and interests, will vary from person to person. Older generations may have had less emphasis on material items and feel comfortable retiring on as little as $3,000 a month (if their fixed costs match current trends). Some people may aspire to a richer lifestyle, including nicer vehicles, more travel, backyard spaces, recreational vehicles; the list goes on. Creating a budget may shed some light on how much your personal household will require to live the retirement lifestyle you desire.

During retirement, you may receive income from Canada Pension Plan (starting at age 60), Old Age Security (starting at age 65), work savings plans, personal savings plans, and even part-time employment. We will concentrate on this final income stream in this chapter. What if your projected retirement income falls short of your lifestyle expenditures? How do you narrow the gap?

Upon reaching desired retirement age, many people, for various reasons, choose to work part time. They may reduce their hours to a couple of days per week or choose seasonal employment. They may seek self-employment, choosing the hours they work, or get a part-time job strictly during the active phase of retirement. To differentiate, I define the active phase as the period, usually at the beginning of retirement, where retirees travel more and enjoy social, busy lives. I define the passive phase as the period, usually later in life, where retirees are a little less active and generally require less income to sustain their lifestyles.

There are many ways to embrace retirement while also creating supplementary income from hobbies and interests. Let's look at some ideas that may resonate with you. In Chapter 3, I tried to note which activities are common ways to supplement income. This list is once again designed to get you thinking. If you are not adept at certain aspects of business or sales, you may outsource these aspects so that you can concentrate exclusively on your unique ability. You will need to consider your start-up costs, such as acquiring the necessary tools and finding the staff or professional services required to get your product or service to market. Can you operate from your present location, or do you need to rent space? Do you need any special permits? There are many aspects to consider when you are running a small business, even part time. Don't be afraid to get professional advice when it comes to the finer details of launching your service.

PHOTOGRAPHY

Photography is a common interest for retirees, and many have learned how to make it profitable. One of the easiest ways to get started is to become a contributor on sites like iStock, Bigstock, and Shutterstock, or to upload your photos to a personal Flickr account and license them through Getty Images. Sites like these may come and go, so investigate the latest.

HOW TO SELL YOUR STOCK PHOTOS:

1. Sign up as a contributor. You'll be required to provide some basic information about yourself, as well as identification documents to prove your identity.

2. Read and familiarize yourself with the submission guidelines.

3. Upload your photos and add metadata, photo descriptions, and relevant keywords.

4. Submit your stock photos for review.

OTHER OPTIONS:

1. You could enter photo contests that offer cash prizes. What do you have to lose? It is not always the seasoned professionals who win these contests. Maybe you have the keen eye required to win. If you are a decent writer or creator, you could start a photography blog or YouTube channel that allows you to offer tutorials, share tips and tricks, or even review products and software.

2. You can apply to freelance job boards that are looking for one-time or ongoing photographers to offer their services.

3. You may be able to sell your photos at art shows and craft fairs.

4. You may be able to land some freelance work for magazines or other publications.

5. You can do photoshoots for individual clients. Many people look for photographers to help document special occasions like the birth of a new baby, Easter and Christmas celebrations, and wedding ceremonies, to name a few. Family photos, boudoir photos, and pet photos are also extremely popular. This option may require an investment in lighting, backdrops, and props.

6. You could work for artists, capturing professional images of their work. Sometimes these photos are used to create professional prints of paintings or sketches.

7. You can supply product photos for online retailers, websites, and print publications.

If you do a little research, you can come up with unique and exciting ways to turn your hobby into some supplementary income. Sometimes, people have enough income to sustain their desired lifestyle and simply need to make enough to cover their travel or hobby costs. Each idea presented here gives you a starting point. You can research what type of equipment you'll need and what costs are involved to make sure you are earning a profit.

WOODWORKING

If you are a decent woodworker, there are endless ways to supplement your retirement income on a schedule that fits your lifestyle. You can even combine your passion with travel and work in your favourite destination. Outsource the business and sales aspects if you wish so that you can spend more time in your shop doing what you love.

You could design and build pieces to be sold at craft shows or online. First, you may want to choose what to specialize in. Are you passionate about cabinetry, furniture, or smaller pieces that can be sold at craft or trade shows? Keep an eye out for local markets as well, and don't forget the viability of online sales. A little research into different online sales platforms could help you gain orders, or you could feature your pieces on your own website. You could also opt to sell your pieces through a specific retailer. If you think making your own website is the right move, but don't know how to set one up, there are endless online resources like YouTube tutorials, and there may be in-person services in your area to assist you. Look into website builders like Wix, Squarespace, Shopify, or GoDaddy and figure out which one best suits your individual needs.

If your woodworking skills include carpentry, you can offer your services to help build fences, decks, or pergolas. You may even be able to make enough money during the summer months to spend your winters abroad.

If you own (or want to purchase) an Alaskan sawmill or bandsaw, you can mill live-edge slabs for residential and commercial use and offer these services to the public. You can take custom orders, make pieces to be used in outdoor spaces, kitchens, bars, or anywhere else people desire wooden surfaces. This is a big undertaking, so consider the cost of the additional tools and resources you may need. Will you need a machine to move logs, or an additional shelter to process your slabs? What about a drying hut, or a vehicle to transport your finished pieces to market? You will also want to account for any noise bylaws that may hinder business in your current location.

Maybe running your own mill seems like more work than you want to take on during retirement. If so, you may decide to work part time for a builder as a framer, trim carpenter, or helper. Your part-time work may even help pay for other hobbies you have. Builders are often frustrated when they cannot secure tradespeople in a timely fashion so being on their rosters can provide extra work. However, you will need to adhere to their schedule and be ready on short notice.

When it comes to woodworking, there are endless ways to supplement your retirement income. Choose a way that is manageable for you and works around your other hobbies and interests. If possible, choose an option that makes use of the tools that you already own so that your capital outlay is minimal and you are not working just to pay for your tools.

COOKING OR BAKING

Many people can't turn down a good meal or their favourite baked good, but some don't have the skills or time necessary to make them. Herein lies the opportunity for the skilled baker or cook. You don't need to work in a restaurant full time to supplement your income. You can create income on a schedule that works around one of your favourite retirement activities.

Personal chefs offer their services in many ways. You can cater events such as birthday parties, backyard gatherings, or other special occasions, choosing events that work with your schedule and offer meals that are within your specialty. Conversely, you may decide to create baked goods to sell at a local market or through an online page or personal website. These options allow you to take as many orders as you are comfortable handling and make as much money as you need to supplement your income. Some people view holidays and special events as potential ways to earn some extra cash through bake sales.

If you have enough dishes that you know well and learn the required computer skills, you can earn money as a food blogger or vlogger. It takes time to develop followers, but once you build your network, you can even branch out to include product endorsements and advertising on your blog. Platforms like YouTube pay once you have a certain number of views and followers on your content. Like blogging, this can branch out to endorsements and advertising revenue. You can use some of your newfound time to research the finer points.

Another option is to teach cooking classes. This can be done small scale in person by getting groups who will pay to sign up. If you are a wine enthusiast, you could even offer classes on cooking and wine pairings. If you do not want to teach classes in person, consider making several cooking videos and combining them into an online course that can be sold to anyone, anywhere in the world. If the written word is more your speed, consider self-publishing your own cookbook with your best recipes. Amazon offers a great platform for authors who wish to self-publish.

Finally, if your passion and knowledge lies in healthy eating, you can develop meal plans for health-minded individuals. Nothing is more confusing for many people than creating a healthy diet that they can stick to long term. If you are good at developing healthy meal plans that are easy to maintain, don't sell yourself short. People will pay for your expertise.

MUSIC

If you are already a decent musician or use the first phase of retirement to really hone your skills, there are many ways to monetize your talent. You can offer music lessons in your home, through a studio, or online. Once you create several pre-recorded lessons, they can be brought together as a course and offered to as many online students as you can attract. If you decide that live music is your passion, you can play at bars, restaurants, festivals, or wineries. A couple of afternoons or evenings per week can add up to some decent extra cash.

You can even get creative and play in your favourite vacation spot if you plan to spend some extended time abroad. Before heading south for the winter, contact the places you hope to play at with your demo or video and try to secure some gigs. Combining two passions, like travel and music, can be a musician's ultimate dream. Instead of forgoing the travel due to lack of funds, find a way to help fund the adventure.

Maybe your musical background allows you to travel with a band or work in a studio. If you aren't working to pay your mortgage or put your kids through school, you can let go of that high-paying job you don't enjoy and trade it for one that feeds your passion.

CONSULTING

Has your former occupation provided the skills necessary to offer consulting services? Consulting at your own pace can be an excellent transition into retirement for those who don't feel ready to retire fully but want to take it down a notch. Working as a consultant on a project-by-project basis can help fill the financial gap while allowing you to ease into retirement a little more slowly. This will help you avoid the feelings of loss I discuss in Chapter 6.

IMPORTANT ASPECTS TO CONSIDER

In today's digital world, there are endless ways to make money online. Still, it may not be as simple as having a web page or You-Tube channel. You need to create solid content to direct traffic to your page. Sometimes, you have to add a layer of creativity. For example, an artist may enjoy painting and simply wish to sell their work. The challenge is getting your paintings out to more than the people who know you or live in your hometown. You might consider dovetailing your love of painting with an online course. As you create your work, video each element for others to learn the skills. Your course followers help create traffic to your site. Eventually, you may get enough followers to warrant endorsements and advertising. Whenever you start a business, much of your success comes from the way you market yourself. Consider adding a unique flare to your course so it attracts a unique audience.

It used to be that your customer base was determined by location. Anyone within a certain distance of your business was a potential customer. If you offered something really unique, your business's reach may expand farther than your hometown and the surrounding area, but the internet has expanded many small business's customer base to the world. However, there are still barriers. You must compete worldwide to attract business from all the other participants in your field.

Marketing creates the conditions where buyers convince themselves to buy your product or service. When you are getting your business off the ground, you may need to devote as much time and energy into marketing as you do into creating your product or service. Luckily the internet is riddled with articles, videos, and courses to teach you the finer points of how to market your work, and discovering these points can be as exciting as seeing their results. Now that you are retired, you have the time to immerse yourself in your creative talents. You may surprise yourself with what you can come up with and have a ton of fun doing it!

NOT EVERYONE IS COMPUTER SAVVY

Not everyone is adept at becoming the next internet sensation or influencer. But you have unique skills and talents; most people do. The goal as a retiree is often to escape the drudgery of waking up to an alarm and commuting to a job you dislike so that you can make enough money to finance your lifestyle. If you have saved enough money to retire and you are just looking to supplement your hobbies or fill in your time with something you enjoy, then concentrate more on the time and less on the money. Use your creativity to figure out how you can offer your product or service a couple days per week, seasonally, or in a few pockets per year. You can still make some money doing something you enjoy while enjoying the freedoms that retirement offers. If you discover your computer talents are limited, consider concentrating on your unique ability and outsourcing the elements, such as computer marketing, to someone who is adept at that part of your business model.

SELF-EMPLOYMENT ISN'T FOR EVERYONE

Okay, time for some tough love. The self-employment route isn't for everyone, and the capital outlay can outweigh the profits. You want to be careful and ensure that your new venture doesn't require more expenditure than you can recuperate with part-time work. Most business owners will tell you that there is a lot more to running a business than meets the eye.

In my experience as a financial planner, I've learned that some-times people think we simply sit back and count our money while the company we work for pays the bills.. The reality is that many financial planners are self employed and pay all their own expenses out of profits. To some, financial planning looks like an easy desk job that doesn't require much work. The reality is quite different.

To run my day-to-day operation, I need to rent an office space, which needs to be furnished with desks, chairs, computers, filing cabinets, and other additions to make the office feel inviting (wall hangings, curtains, plants, warm lighting, etc.), as well as minor renovations to make the space my own. All of this is usually at the business owner's expense. On top of that, you need to pay industry fees such as licensing, bonding, liability insurance, regulatory fees, and legal and accounting fees that can easily add up to thousands of dollars per month. You need office machines, paper, ink, the list goes on. You have utility bills, staff wages, tax remittances, and a host of other expenses big and small. When you get started, you have exactly zero clients. Each new relationship is developed painstakingly, one client at a time. Some marketing efforts bring in new business while others simply fail, but in both cases the expense is there. That moment of seemingly spontaneous success comes after late nights, rejections, criticism, doubts, risks, discipline, and disappointment.

None of this is meant to sound like one long complaint. It is meant to remind you that if people look like they are making easy money, it is highly likely that they have worked long and hard to get to the point where it appears that way. A friend of mine has a great saying when people tell her she is lucky to have what she has. She responds, "It's funny. The harder I work, the luckier I get." Nothing could sum it up better.

There is another old saying that states that you should not be jealous of others who have what you don't; they simply did what you won't, completed what you quit, started what you wouldn't try, and made the sacrifices you wouldn't. These are all ways that hard-working entrepreneurs are trying to communicate that the journey to success is a long difficult one and you must think about this journey before jumping into a new venture.

If the idea is to supplement your retirement income, you want to be careful that you are not simply creating an extra expense. If your new venture requires you to outlay $25,000 in tools and expenses to get started, ask yourself if you can reasonably make that money back. After working and giving your all for years, do you have it in you to start a new venture that may require your all to get it going? The last thing I want to do is encourage a venture to supplement income that results in you going into debt instead.

You know yourself best. Work within your comfort zones, skill sets, and desired time constraints. You have worked hard to get to this level of freedom. Make sure you are getting the most out of it. Part-time work, seasonal retirement gigs, and side hustles should be a fun way to make some extra money, not a point of stress in your world. I'd like to leave you with one last idea to fill in financial gaps that doesn't require traditional work.

ACCESSING HOME EQUITY

If you have planned well enough to retire with no mortgage and still live in your family home, you may have an opportunity in front of you. Many people have a desire to travel extensively but are uncomfortable leaving their home empty or renting it out. Secondly, it may be difficult to afford this kind of lifestyle on top of all your household expenses.

One option is to sell the house and invest the proceeds in a safer income portfolio designed to earn a steady 6% to 6.5% with little risk to your principle. It is worth noting that investing the proceeds in a single stock, a small group of stocks, crypto currency, precious metal, or risk assets is not a sound investment strategy. Use a trusted independent financial advisor to put together a diversified income portfolio aimed at producing a steady monthly payout without significant risk to your capital. This money will be held in a separate account from your other assets. Consider maximizing your TFSA (Tax Free Savings Account) and investing the remainder in a non-registered plan. The goal is to create a steady stream of income to pay for your travels not to hit a home run on a speculative asset.

Let's look at an example. A couple decides to sell their large family home and receives $700,000 after paying all expenses associated with the sale. They consult a trusted independent financial planner who shows them a solid income-balanced portfolio that has produced a return of 6.5% net of all fees since its inception. Their financial planner sets up a monthly plan whereby the couple receives $3,208 per month, representing a distribution of 5.5%. ($700,000 x 0.055 = $38,500 per year or $3,208 per month). This money is in addition to the steady retirement income they already receive from their government, work pensions, and personal savings plans. They decide that they wish to travel for one year, and this additional $3,208 per month covers their extra costs such as lodging and transportation. Their other income pays for their day-to-day lifestyle. They have virtually no fixed monthly costs back home as they have sold their home and all the expenses that go with it. Whether they buy groceries at home or in another country the cost is similar. They are not making car payments, insurance, or gas back home either.

Throughout the year, they choose several bucket-list destinations to visit, staying several weeks in each so that they can experience their travels at a pace they enjoy. They have never been able to take more than two weeks vacation before due to their obligations back home. In some countries, they find it best to rent Airbnb accommodations. They learn that some Airbnb hosts offer discounts for lengthier stays of several weeks (after all, the host is not paying cleaning fees every few days or doing the work required to rent to several guests over the same timespan). In other countries, the couple decides to phone a travel company and negotiate a flat rate for several weeks at an all-inclusive resort. Since there is only one round-trip flight involved, the weeks in between are cheaper, and since the resort includes food and drinks, their monthly cost isn't significantly different than staying at an Airbnb, where they paid for all their food and drinks separately.

Throughout the year, they visit a total of 10 countries. This form of travel gives them the chance to immerse themselves in the local culture of each, rather than seeing only the major sights at a shotgun pace. Before departing, they check with their provincial healthcare provider about extended travel away from Canada so that they maintain coverage when they return home. When our couple returns to Canada, they cash out this investment plan and purchase a smaller house suitable for their retirement years. They pay cash and leave some money aside for the income tax they will pay on the gains they used for income. Since the investment earned 6.5% and they only used 5.5%, their portfolio is worth $707,000.00 at the end of this wonderful year. Keep in mind, they were only spending the gains and the original capital is intact at year end.

Now, of course, this investment is not guaranteed. The risk involved is that their investment underperforms during this year. It is important to work with your advisor and try to plan this type of adventure when market conditions are most favorable. It is also not advisable to invest in a riskier portfolio in an attempt to have more money when you return. This can easily backfire on you. If markets experienced more volatility than you hoped, you could choose a short-term rental option upon returning until markets bring your portfolio back to even. That could take six months to a year or even more. For most people, this would be the adventure of a lifetime, so you must decide if you are prepared to deal with the inherent risks.

CHAPTER 5

THE PHASES OF RETIREMENT

WHILE THERE ARE varying views on how many phases of retirement there are and what they are called, certain common elements seem to emerge for many people. The amount of time a retiree may spend in these phases and the struggles or triumphs they may experience along the way are unique to each individual. During these phases, you will likely see your retirement personality, as discussed in Chapter 2, start to emerge.

PHASE 1 – PRE-RETIREMENT

Pre-retirement generally encompasses the four to five years leading up to retirement. For the goal-oriented or Adventurer, this is the stage where they begin to mentally shift from earlier life goals like raising a family, achieving success in their career, or building that dream home. This is when they begin longing to reconnect with their more personal goals. You may find yourself focusing on getting your ducks in order and researching many of the things discussed in Chapter 1. This can be a time of great excitement and anticipation, but it also may elicit feelings of anxiety. It is important to remember that you are the author of your own story. Why not make it a great one? For the Leisure Seeker, this phase can feel like a countdown to freedom and a slower pace that allows them to take life day by day.

During the covid-19 pandemic, we began to see an increase in mental health disorders, alcohol and drug abuse, and strained relationships. While getting your finances in order is essential to retiring comfortably, I cannot stress enough that it is equally important to have your mental health and quality of relationships in check. During lockdowns and sustained periods of working from home, many couples discovered things about their partners that got on their nerves. Many people also discovered their own demons. I once heard it said that you either emerged from the pandemic a hunk, a chunk, or a drunk. If nothing else, being removed from society and spending all our extra time with our families taught us a lot about our shortcomings. We are all human, and none of us are immune to life's challenges. If we are to create the glorious retirement we long for, it may require a little work on ourselves in advance.

As much as they may not want to admit it, North Americans can easily hide behind their busy hectic lifestyles. A lot of things about us can easily get swept under the rug. The more time you spend working on yourself and your relationships during this phase, the greater the likelihood that you'll achieve the glorious retirement you hoped for when purchasing this guide. If you have recently discovered that you and your partner really don't have as much in common as you hoped, this may be a good time to ask yourself some hard questions and work on your relationship. After all, you are about to possibly spend another 40-plus hours per week with your partner. How you choose to address the quality of your romantic relationship is entirely up to you, but choosing to ignore present problems may make the next phase of your retirement very tumultuous.

A little introspection and examination of your mental and emotional processes is essential during this phase. You may come to the realization that you would benefit from counselling or another form of self-improvement. When we choose to allocate a little time and money to self-improvement and growth, we have the potential to discover a host of things that we were unaware that we brought to our relationships. This is simply part of the human condition. For some, counselling takes the form of weekly sessions with a therapist. While this can be costly, it can also uncover the things we need to improve, bringing about quicker results. For others, this process may involve using books or online resources and courses to fine tune some of the things that create conflict in their relationships.

In some households, working on self-improvement as a couple is a much more effective way to reduce conflict and improve the overall quality of their relationship. A relationship is not a place we go to get something but rather a place we go to give something. Albeit a humbling experience, we must be willing to assess and work on some of the toxic traits we have picked up as we navigated all the struggles that life has thrown our way. Achieving overall peace of mind is a key ingredient in truly enjoying our new retirement journey.

While these concepts can certainly improve our romantic relationships, they also apply to our friendships. Not everyone's life journey is the same. You may discover that retirement is yet another major life change that makes you assess your current friendships and even make the difficult decision to leave some behind. There will always be people who are simply jealous that you are retiring, while they are not. It's important that you stay focused on the goal of creating the retirement you have worked your whole life to enjoy. For those who decide to retire to a different location, the move itself may necessitate new friendships.

For retirees whose major goal is a slower pace, creating comfortable spaces with people they enjoy being around or what the Danish people call hygge (pronounced something like \hew-guh\) may be a top priority. This phase is an excellent time to think about starting to create the comfortable spaces that you may enjoy during retirement, especially if you identify with the Leisure Seeker personality. We often think of the retired woman who converts her child's old bedroom into a sewing room or the man who converts the garage into a workshop, but these activities need not be gender specific. When it comes to *hygge*, we may think of the avid reader who turns an old shed or room into a warm and inviting reading nook. Or the couple who creates a backyard oasis to entertain friends.

PHASE 2 – THE HONEYMOON PHASE

When the day you retire finally comes, it can elicit a lot of emotions. Some people may be in shock, having thought this day would never arrive, while others may feel a sense of loss as they leave friends and colleagues behind. It is not uncommon for tears of both joy and sadness to be shed. This is a day of great significance. For many, it holds the same weight as the day they graduated from college or university, the day they got married, or the day their child was born. It can elicit a whirlwind of strong emotions.

How you choose to celebrate this day can play a significant role in the beginning of this new journey. You may wish to give some thought to how you will close this chapter and how you want to start the next. Some are fortunate to have colleagues, friends, or family throw a big party. Those who worked in law enforcement or fire prevention may participate in something more ceremonious like a salute of gratitude.

Unfortunately, not all people move to retirement of their own free will. Some are forced out of a job and have feelings of resentment. For these people, a period of reflection and healing may need to take place before any grand plans are put into effect. If your circle is small and big celebrations make you uncomfortable, you may come up with a much more intimate way of celebrating this grand achievement or recovering from this loss. However, as this day unfolds, try to put some thought into how to make it a day of positivity, a cathartic release or quite simply the beginning of a new chapter that you get to design for yourself.

This book is dedicated to creating a happy retirement. Whatever that means to you, do your best to come up with a plan that feels glorious. Hopefully, the reason you retired is that you have enough passive income to survive, perhaps with a decent nest egg on top. You have been liberated from the stresses of the working world and can enjoy your time, relationships, purpose, and financial freedom.

Time is something you have at your disposal during the Honeymoon Phase. All those projects you put off because you didn't have the time to pursue them can suddenly become a reality. Some retirees suddenly become models of productivity during this euphoric phase. Others choose to take the extended vacation of their dreams whether that be a flight to an exotic location, an extended road trip, or a lengthy stay in a mountain cabin. For most North Americans, vacation time is a sparse commodity. The freedom of time allows your dreams to come true. This is also the phase where we have the opportunity to dive deep into our hobbies and interests, taking these passions to a new level. Remember those goals you cast aside due to lack of time? Now is the time to make them happen.

Retirement can also become a time to deepen your relationships, romantic or otherwise. Retirees often love the chance to visit their children or grandchildren, cherishing that quality time. They may find the quality of their friendships improves, especially if those friends are also retired. Retiring to communities that cater to people in this age group brings about amazing social connections with people of a similar mindset. Having time to spend with our partner can either bring about a deeper connection or highlight pre-existing problems. If you didn't tend to relationship issues before retirement, it may be time to now. They say that families that play together, stay together. If you are lucky enough to have a partner who shares similar interests, your relationship may begin to flourish in new ways.

Not everyone defines themselves by what they do for a living or gains a huge sense of purpose from their work. Removing those shackles can open a world of opportunity. Retirement may be your time to shine. Whether you choose to launch a business, become an active volunteer or mentor, write that book, or dive deep into a hobby or interest, you have an opportunity to create a sense of purpose.

Loss of purpose is one of the retirement losses I discuss in Chapter 6. Whether you allow this redefinition of purpose to become a freedom or a loss is up to you. Even if your work or business played a huge role in your life and you felt it defined who you were, you can view retirement as your next career and approach your leisure activities with the same fervour you devoted to your work. Let's face it, when we meet someone, one of the first questions they ask is what we do for a living. When someone asks what you do for a living now, say, "Whatever the heck I want!" Joking aside, if you retire at a young age, you will get asked over and over about what you do with your time. Having an answer ready will make those conversations much smoother. Or you can simply recommend those people read this book!

Working as an independent financial planner has given me the opportunity to guide many families through a process that ultimately led them to financial freedom. If you have planned accordingly and are going into retirement with little or no debt, you will have some basic fixed costs such property tax, gas and hydro, phone, internet, tv, and car and home insurance. You may have rent or a car payment. The rest of your income can be used to design a lifestyle.

Chapter 3 got you thinking about what you want to do with your time. This is the phase where you get to do it. If you plan carefully, you should be able to acquire all the tools necessary to enjoy your hobbies or interests and plan at least a few vacations. A lot of people ask how retirees get by on an income that is lower than what they used to make. The reality is a lot of pre-retirement expenses will disappear at this stage of your life. Hopefully, your mortgage payment will cease before you retire. If you have planned well, so will your debt payments. For most households, those two alone represent a large figure. If you had children and they are grown, you can eliminate or reduce those expenses as well. Whether its diapers and formula, sports and activities, post-secondary education, weddings, or financial assistance, there comes a time when these expenses are significantly reduced or eliminated.

By retirement, most people have their homes set up. You won't likely be buying major furniture, TVs, patio sets, or lawn equipment unless you choose to upgrade one at a time. Lastly, you won't be investing into RRSP and TFSA accounts every year anymore. The point is, even if you are carrying debt or a car payment or both, the size and number of expenses should be significantly less that when you were at the peak of financial responsibility. I picture the financial timeline from your 20s to your 60s as a triangle. In our early 20s, most of our lives are pretty simple and lower key. As we reach our 30s, it is common to buy houses and raise families, creating more complexity and greater expense. Eventually, you reach a peak, after which expenses start to disappear.

A person's retirement often coincides with the point in their lives when they have created enough passive income to fuel their current lifestyle. This is when a person is said to have freedom of money. Despite these freedoms, this Honeymoon Phase fizzles out for a lot of people. It is not that different from a new relationship. While it may be true that people can stay in this stage for many years or even decades, things in life evolve and we grow during each phase of our lives. If we went a little too crazy at the beginning or didn't have an independent financial planner to guide us with portfolio management, we may find that a declining portfolio gets us to the next phase quicker than we hoped.

PHASE 3 – AGING AND FEELING INSIGNIFICANT

Unfortunately for many or even most of us, not all of the retirement phases are wonderful. It is not uncommon to reach a, "Now what?" phase. If you aren't a detailed planner or didn't get retirement advice when you were younger, the Honeymoon Phase might have been much like that of a typical university student who used their newfound freedom to go a little wild. Wild usually entails different activities in our later years, but the concept is similar. Woo-hoo, vacation, project, project, vacation, hobby, hobby, my back is getting sore, funds are depleting ... now what? When the euphoria wears off, the losses described in Chapter 6 can set in.

In some cases, it's age that slows us down; in others, it's depleting funds or the feeling of insignificance. The realization that you are, in fact, getting older, that your time on Earth is diminishing and the busy working people all around you just don't have time to fit you in their lives. Don't fret. All is not a lost. You can move to the next phase. What is important in this phase is to navigate the losses carefully and concentrate on the freedoms outlined in the Honeymoon Phase.

Some people take on a part-time job at this point. They may not need extra income. They may just need something to occupy their time and facilitate new social interactions. It may be that after a lifetime of structure, discipline, and deadlines, we just don't know how to manage our free time. This is a great time to reread Chapter 2 and 3 to get new ideas about how to fill the void. In any event, with some careful consideration you can move on to the next phase.

PHASE 4 – REINVENTING YOURSELF

Some of the successful retirees I know worked their way through several retirement personalities or their own distinct phases. Even if they reached pockets of insignificance, they knew how to quickly get back to living life. During the first phase, they may have wound down and completed projects, associating more with the Leisure Seeker personality type. When they achieved more inner peace, they may have moved on to a Jet Setter phase. Next, they may have become a bit of a Searcher as they tried different activities or even decided to spend some time abroad.

You may have heard of the movie *The Bucket List*. If your bucket list is long enough, it can take years or even decades to assemble and work through all the items on your personal list. For those who aren't familiar, the concept is to create a list of things you wish to try or accomplish before you "kick the bucket." For some, reinventing yourself might mean taking it easy and enjoying some simple pleasures. Others may already be off to their next adventure. Not everyone's retirement will be associated with free, untouched time. Grandparents do babysit grandkids and sometimes aging parents require care. If I can offer any advice from my research, it's this: When life isn't dictating your time for you, try your best to fill it with things that you find productive and fulfilling.

PHASE 5 – STABILITY

Not everyone will reach this phase. Let's face it, life throws a lot of curve balls at us, and the average person navigates a lot of struggles during their time on Earth. However, if you are fortunate enough to have planned your finances well and have been graced with good health, you may reach this final stage. Phase 5 can be seen as a gift that allows us to leave our mark on the world. It can be a phase to make peace with your mistakes, enjoy lasting relationships, and even create a legacy. When you reach this phase, hopefully you have forged a life of simplicity. Maybe you can look back at a good working life and the achievement of some personal goals along the way such as buying or building a home, raising a family, or living a life full of adventure. You can probably create a list of the pleasurable experiences you have enjoyed.

In later-stage retirement, you may have created a way to give something back to the world. Not every charitable act must happen on a grand scale and be posted about on social media. Sometimes, we simply help out family and friends or pay a kindness to a stranger. If these things haven't been a regular occurrence in your life, this may be a great phase to help the next ones along. Your legacy may be that you wrote a book, created one or more works of art, mentored someone, or raised one or more children who turned out to be good human beings. A big part of this phase is looking back with contentment, a sense of inner peace, and a feeling of accomplishment.

If you have worked hard enough to achieve financial independence, you have earned the right to do what you want with your time and money. Many studies show that we achieve greater happiness by giving to others than by receiving from them. Studies have also shown that the good feeling in giving to others lasts longer. If you were given $50 per day to either spend on yourself or give to another, the pleasure of spending on ourselves diminishes much quicker than the pleasure in giving to another. Some of the unhappiest retirees turn out to be those that have never advanced beyond pleasing themselves.

SUMMARY

By utilizing this guide to develop and rework your personal retirement timeline, you increase your chances of looking back on your life and enjoying a feeling of accomplishment, all while experiencing a happy retirement! These phases are not always linear in nature. It is natural to move back and forth through these stages and still experience struggles along the way. Successful relationships get messy at times, things don't always go as planned, financial markets don't go up in straight line, and your health may not always be the greatest. People plateau, get stuck in phases, or revert to earlier ones along the way. Most people who have achieved success in one or more areas of their life will agree on the benefits of making and following a plan. Many companies mandate schedules, sales projections, and other planning tools because they get results. Retirement is no different. Taking the time to set some goals and create a plan of action will certainly increase your chances of achieving more of the things on your personal bucket list and increase your overall satisfaction.

CHAPTER 6

DEALING WITH THE LOSSES
THAT MAY OCCUR

MEETING WITH FINANCIAL planning clients over the years, I have always been fascinated by the number of people who cannot picture what to do with their time during retirement and quite frankly seem fearful of the idea. Western culture has conditioned us from a young age to get a job, work hard, and take little vacation time. Some people wear their time at work as a badge of honour. They equate hard work and long hours with being a stronger, better person. After all, these are the principles North Americans are taught from a young age. We are slowly moving away from this concept, and time is becoming a currency in itself. Nonetheless, when a person does decide to retire, it is very common for them to experience one or more losses. Let's review these losses and see if we can prepare ourselves for them in advance.

Why do we feel a sense of loss in the first place? Studies have shown that as many as 40% of retirees experience a sense of loss or feelings of depression when they retire. However, the number of people still working at 65 who experience feelings of depression are very similar. In either case, there is a likelihood that this milestone causes us to reflect on the choices we have made in the past. It is highly likely that we may regret some of the choices we have made over the years. We may even feel we have not lived up to our potential. Human beings are creatures of habit. We get used to the patterns in our lives. When we experience a death, the loss of a loved one, or even retirement from a lengthy occupation, the stages of grief follow. This is perfectly normal, and it is best to accept that you will experience these feelings. But what do we do about them?

What if we reframe our situation? What if we look at retirement from the lens of gratitude and with a growth mindset? When New Year's rolls around, many of us make a list of resolutions for the new year. We reflect on the past year and consider what we would like to do differently. Retirement is simply a new chapter in our lives, and it can be a different and better chapter. You can choose to write a future that is better than your past because you get to write this chapter with a lifetime of experience behind you. You are not starting from square one. You have already learned the hard life lessons you need to advance to the next stage.

At some point in your life, it is possible that you or someone you know may have felt like starting over in a new location, transitioning to a new job, or exploring a new relationship. Some have wondered what they could accomplish if they liquidated everything they have with their current net worth. If your current net worth was sitting in an account and you could start creating the life of your dreams, where would you begin? Where would your home be and what kind of home would you live in? What car would you drive? Where would you travel to? What hobbies and interests would you enjoy? What could you do without and what would you leave behind? This is the opportunity that retirement gives to each of us.

There is a psychological exercise that asks you to write your own eulogy. Writing what you hope others would say about you helps solidify the kind of life that truly matters to you and gives you the tools to live the life you want to now. Likewise, if you were to look back on your retirement three years in, what would have to have happened for you to feel that your first 3 years had been a raging success? The answer to this will tell you what you need to accomplish.

You may also want to do a Strength, Weakness, Opportunity, Threat (SWOT) Analysis and consider what strengths, weaknesses, opportunities, and threats have the potential to affect your plan. Considering these weaknesses and threats should not fuel excuses for why your retirement plans won't work. Instead, they can provide a realistic assessment of the obstacles that need to be considered and the skills necessary to bring about the ultimate success of your plan. Do you have the financial resources to fulfill this master plan? If not, prioritize the things that are most important to you and consider what you can live without.

Once you have clarified what you can and cannot live without, write a realistic plan to achieve your retirement goals. Remember that you don't jump straight to the top of a mountain but rather take one purposeful step at a time. The Japanese have a concept called *Kaizen*, which roughly translates to continuous improvement. Once your ultimate dream plan is written down, try to take one small step in the right direction every week. This probably sounds like a lot of work, but so is everything else in life that is worth attaining. If the ultimate retirement is what you seek, then you simply apply the same principles that bring about success in any business, relationship, or personal endeavour.

Let's take a closer look at the typical losses retirees experience and how you can navigate them.

LOSS OF IDENTITY

When we meet someone new, one of the first questions they invariably ask is what we do for a living. This information allows people to size us up and formulate a mental picture of who we are. In our capitalist society, the answer to this question is often an important indicator of how the conversation will proceed. Beneath the surface lie sub questions such as how much money do you make? Do you make more than me? What is your socio-economic status? How should I judge you? Can you help me in any way?

Beyond how others see us, our identity can be strongly linked to how we see ourselves through the lens of what we do for a living. If we consider a teacher for example, they often formulate a bond with their students by connecting with them intellectually. They spend a significant amount of time each day interacting with students during a period in which they learn and grow as individuals. Many of the good ones are known for making a huge impact on the lives of these individuals. In a few cases they may even guide them through a difficulty they are experiencing in life or help to provide direction in their futures. So, naturally, when they are no longer in this role, they can experience a loss of who they are and what they offer to this world.

Grief is a natural and often painful response to this kind of loss. You have likely heard of the five stages of grief as outlined by psychiatrist Elisabeth Kubler-Ross: denial, anger, bargaining, depression, and acceptance. Retirement is a major life change and sometimes happens quite quickly, making it difficult for many people to experience. If we mentally prepare in advance, however, we are better equipped to navigate this inevitable feeling of loss.

Imagine being asked what you do at a party and answering, "I'm a jet setter," or, "I'm an artist." They would likely pull up a chair and undoubtedly want to know more. As I have said many times throughout this book, if we don't see ourselves as retiring from something but rather to something, our concept of retirement takes on a new sense of purpose. People can explore several careers in their lifetime. Viewing retirement as one of these careers can prove useful, especially for those who are hesitant to leave their working life behind. After all, retirement is a big accomplishment that is not afforded to everyone. As we discussed in Chapter 5, it is important in the pre-retirement stage to get your emotional house in order. This may mean mentally reframing what you are going through and viewing it as a huge gift of freedom. If you are already retired, you can still reframe how you view this loss and see your retirement for the huge gain it is!

You are not defined by what you do for a living. You are a father, a mother, a son, a daughter, a friend, a confidant. You are more about how you treat the world around you. You are about your core values, beliefs, and morals. As the old saying goes, "Many things in life will catch your eye; a few will capture your heart." Pursue the things that capture your heart. If you find yourself searching for a new identity after retirement, consider what moves you in this world.

LOSS OF STRUCTURE

During our working lives, we may question exactly how we are going to fulfill all the commitments that land on our busy plates. Regardless, the structure of a working lifestyle often becomes a part of who we are. Most of us adhere to some sort of schedule to complete our work tasks, school tasks, family tasks, etc. Families with kids often find themselves devoting a lot of time to sports, activities, and social obligations. When we retire, filling our schedules with other activities can create a challenge for many people, especially those who haven't created a plan for their retirement. This loss of structure can weigh on some people and make them feel rather empty.

This is especially true for individuals who aren't used to including their own hobbies, interests, and physical activities in their busy schedules. If you used to work, then go home and just relax, then retiring may take away the main element of structure you had in your life. For the Leisure Seeker, this may be the welcome change that they have been yearning for. But eventually, if you don't replace the time you spent working, with something else, the gift of free time can easily turn into boredom.

If this loss of structure hits you rather hard, the real problem may be that you haven't developed enough personal interests in your adult life. Let's face it, working and raising a family can easily consume most of our time. Many parents prioritize their children's interests, giving up their free time to nurture their children's passions whether that be sports, dance, clubs, gymnastics, or other activities. They may say things like, "I wouldn't dream of enjoying a sport or activity with my schedule." Well, if you're retired, it may be time for a little introspection. Hopefully reading through Chapter 3 sparked a few ideas. Picking one or two main activities and scheduling them into your weekly routine is a good place to start.

If you are picking up a new activity, it may require you to acquire a few tools for your craft and even develop some new skills. Developing new skills is often the real stumbling block for people, but we must get past the idea that it is too late to start something new. It can be very inspiring seeing how many people such as actors, athletes, and authors have achieved greatness at a later stage in life. You may find that your new activity is rather tiring at an older age, and it may be time to incorporate some health and fitness into your weekly routine as well. You may need to do a bit of reading or attend an online or in-person class to foster your knowledge and increase your skill set. Before you know it, your avocation and all the activities that accompany it can create the structure you have been missing.

Whatever route you choose, action is the key to getting over this loss. It doesn't matter if you don't stay with it. You may try several different paths before settling into the one that resonates with you. The key is to start by trying one.

LOSS OF PURPOSE

We may struggle with our sense of purpose more than once as we move through the different phases of our lives. The struggle to find purpose is often cited as one that retirees feel most acutely. Delving too deep into existential questions about our place in the world has the potential to leave us mentally drained or depressed, so try to focus on your personal sense of purpose and what brings you joy. Society may teach us that our purpose is to get married and have kids, or that we should find meaning in how much money we earn or the achievement of a certain status or title. But these things will often not fulfill your real personal sense of purpose.

"I'm retired," you may say. "Now what?" Understanding your significance in this world can come from answering two questions: *Who am I?* and *Why do I exist?* The first question speaks to your sense of personal identity, and the second speaks to the question of purpose. While we are often taught that our purpose is linked to how we make money, I believe our purpose is much greater. If we view our purpose as something outside of our careers, leaving our employment and the feelings of loss that come with it are merely stepping stones to a greater sense of purpose.

Retirement can provide the slower pace necessary to ponder the question of why we exist and decide what is important to us at this stage of our lives. We have discussed the idea that retirement can elicit some of our shortcomings and make us come to terms with things we may need to improve about ourselves and our relationships. If you allocate some time and energy to personal growth, it may give you the chance to create a new sense of purpose based on what is nearest and dearest to your heart. If you cannot decide what you are passionate about, try asking your friends and family. They are likely to tell you what they have observed about you without overthinking these questions.

A great exercise is to take a blank page and list all of the wonderful experiences you've had in your life. Instead of always goal setting for the future, it can be cathartic to look back on the things we are proud to have already accomplished. Think about the challenges you have faced along the way. Once you have completed this exercise, you can look at the result and realize that in spite of all the challenges you have faced in your life, you have managed to create some truly wonderful experiences. This realization should give you some insight into what brings you joy and fulfillment.

What experiences have you put off because you just couldn't find the time for them? Is there a skill you always wished you had that could make a difference in your life or in the lives of others? Is there a relationship with a family member or friend that you would like to repair? Purpose doesn't have to be an end goal so much as something that impacts the world around us. We often get a greater sense of purpose from what we give to the world than what we take from it. Purpose is your long-term reason for getting out of bed each day and blends with the things that bring you joy and a sense of fulfillment. If a gift or skill you possess leads to something greater, it can help promote better physical and mental health, as well as a strong sense of identity.

If the loss of purpose is something that you are really struggling with, now may be a good time to consider counselling. You don't want to waste years of your life wandering aimlessly without a sense of purpose. Regardless, don't let your sense of purpose or lack thereof prevent your happiness. Your purpose can change and evolve throughout your life so adopting a growth mindset is one of the best ways to manage this sense of loss.

LOSS OF RELATIONSHIPS

We spend so much time at our jobs and create some great long-lasting relationships as a result. When we retire, we may move to a new location or simply to a new phase of our lives. Talking to old friends who have not yet retired about the wonderful lives we have created as retirees can lead to jealousy or simply a lack of understanding.

Sometimes, entering a new stage of life simply means drifting away from those who knew us before. Whenever we end a long-term relationship, it can leave us feeling empty and even a little lonely. The fact is, as a retiree, you are going to have a lot more free time. Occasions to meet up with work friends will be limited to the free time their busy lifestyles afford them. If you are used to being surrounded by a large group that socializes while they get their work done, you may find the silence deafening.

However, this doesn't have to be a total loss. As you settle into your new routine and start focusing on the activities that you have decided to prioritize, you will come across people in a similar situation who share similar interests. This doesn't mean you will never see your work friends again, but you may naturally develop some new relationships as well.

Consider the Jet Setter who decides to do a group trip through a travel club. Spending a week or two away enjoying a beautiful location is bound to create some camaraderie with the other passengers. It is not uncommon for the people you meet during travel to contact you once you return home. Some travellers find that these new friends end up being a travel family whom they travel with many times.

If your retirement personality aligns with the Athlete, you may find yourself meeting with other people who share your passion. Perhaps you will end up joining a group of cyclists, for example. A quick internet search can lead you to local groups who meet up to cycle regularly. These groups may even offer group vacations where they see their desired locations mainly on two wheels. You may end up seeing the same people at bike shops or cycling a local path. Whatever your sport is, birds of a feather will flock together.

Life changes will bring about new relationships. Whether it's moving to a new town, a new school, a new employer, or entering retirement, making new friends can be fun!

LOSS OF POWER

Depending on what you did for a living, you may have experienced a certain amount of power, influence, or admiration. This kind of power can be a real confidence booster. For example, if you worked in IT or a trade, you likely had frantic people coming to you regularly to solve complex problems. When you solved these problems, you could see the relief they experienced. If you worked as an accountant, lawyer, or teacher, people may have relied heavily upon you for advice. If you were in sales, you may have been the resident expert on a product or service. Whatever you did to earn a living, you may have derived a certain sense of power or control from your work.

When you are no longer active in this capacity, it can lead to feelings of insignificance. Retirees and seniors are sometimes unfairly viewed as past their prime. Given how quickly things evolve these days, they may no longer be considered an expert in their industry and people may even take their advice less seriously.

As we move many years into retirement, we must also face the inevitable factors associated with aging. We may experience diminished mental capacity or feel that our opinions are taken less seriously. One of the reasons men are recorded as having a higher rate of depression during retirement is due to the ingrained gender roles our society places upon them. Though not exclusive to men, being seen as a family provider is still prevalent in modern gender roles. Once we stop working and move into retirement, this can easily add to the losses we experience. The self-worth we feel from being gainfully employed is something that is often overlooked until we are no longer working, and feelings of loss arise.

If you struggle with this form of loss, you may find it helpful to concentrate on the enormous accomplishment of achieving the level of financial independence that allowed you to retire in the first place. Try to view freedom as a different and exciting new power.

SUMMARY

Navigating and overcoming feelings of loss requires action and a growth mindset. You must decide that you want to be happy if you desire a happy retirement. Then take the first step and create a plan. Use the accompanying workbook to help you complete this task. Next, put your plan into motion. If any of these steps pose roadblocks that you can't seem to get past, seek out some guidance.

Do you need a counsellor or coach? If you view retirement as your next career move, then you may find the skills of a career counsellor helpful. Most counselling and coaching professionals don't solve your problems for you. Instead, they help you organize your thoughts in such a way that you come to the right decision on your own. Life coaches ask questions. They may try to help you reframe negative thoughts or excuses and give you the gentle push you need to make the right decisions. Sometimes, they offer tools and resources to help you overcome your current struggles.

The problem is never the problem. The problem is that we don't know how to think about the problem. The solution usually lies in seeing things from a place of gratitude and with a growth mindset.

CONCLUSION

AS I CHECK back in from time to time on the retired client from the introduction, she still has that serenity and peace of mind she had been searching for when she planned her retirement. Her smile is a little bigger these days. I am confident that her preparedness has set her in the right direction toward a glorious retirement. She will undoubtedly experience a few different phases along the way, but she has found her happy place.

Hopefully, as you made your way through this book, you uncovered your own personal barriers to retirement and answered a lot of the questions you had about how to transition into this new and exciting stage of life. If you used the accompanying workbook, you have laid the groundwork for creating an excellent retirement lifestyle plan specialized to your specific needs.

In Chapter 1, we began by discussing the mechanical aspects of the process in the years leading up to your retirement. I hope you have gained a clearer picture of where you hope to live, what purchases you may need to make in the years leading up to retirement, and what expenses you may need to tend to while you are still working. If you are already retired, I hope you have gathered some new ideas that steer you toward the happiness and peace of mind you desire.

In Chapter 2, we covered the nine typical retirement personalities to get you to identify what you truly want. Identifying your retirement personality is important as it allows you to focus on what truly brings you happiness in this world and gives you the tools necessary to put your dream retirement plan in motion. Whether you are a Leisure Seeker or Adventurer, an Artist or an Athlete, the possibilities of how you spend your days, weeks, and years are endless. When you are certain of what makes you feel alive, you can use your newfound freedom to explore and make the most of your experiences.

Occupying the time that you used to devote to work and work-related activities is a common struggle. I truly hope that Chapter 3 got your creative juices flowing and helped you create a life you can't wait to wake up to and experience each day. Giving yourself permission to fill your days with activities that you truly enjoy is a key element in this process. Filling in your activity chart is another key to feeling fulfilled during your retirement years. Lastly, we discussed several ideas to help you plan your vacation time and get the most out of your travels. Whether it's a weekend getaway or winters abroad, there are many ways to turn a simple trip into an adventure that makes you feel alive!

If you were worried about whether you have saved enough to retire on, I hope that Chapter 4 provided some useful guidance. There are endless ways to turn one of your hobbies or interests into additional retirement income. The goal is to work at something you enjoy. Use one of the ideas presented or create your own. Set up additional income streams that don't interfere with your ability to do what you truly love. For some, a retirement venture becomes an integral element in their plan that brings them great joy and a sense of purpose. Enjoy the journey and make it part of your retirement process. Embrace learning and all the victories and mistakes that come with it. You are the creator of your own life, so why not create something wonderful?

Chapter 5 covered the typical phases of retirement. Everyone goes through these phases to some degree. Recognize the psychological aspects that can create challenges for most individuals. Utilize the tools and suggestions presented to help you navigate these challenges. View this book as a reference tool to revisit when your retirement is feeling a little less than glorious. Look over the notes you made in the accompanying workbook to remind you of what you truly want for yourself, then get back on track.

Finally, in Chapter 6, we covered the five typical losses that occur: the loss of identity, the loss of structure, the loss of purpose, the loss of relationships, and the loss of power. Much like the stages of grief, these feelings of loss are a natural part of making the leap into retirement. Keeping this book as a reference point and rereading your notes should help keep you on track. Use these resources as a springboard to work on the areas you struggle with and find your way back to your plan. Your workbook can serve as a key tool to get you back on track quickly.

The challenges and negative aspects of life can often feel like they outweigh the joys. Embrace the concept of Kaizen so that you are always advancing in the direction of your dreams. What is the next step in your dream plan? Remember that navigating and overcoming feelings of loss requires action and a growth mindset. You must decide you want to be happy and create a glorious retirement.

Once you have made this commitment, all you need to do is take the next step in the plan you created.

I sincerely hope that you have gained a greater appreciation of what it takes to create the retirement lifestyle of your dreams. I have spent most of my adult life guiding my valued clients through this process, and I hope this book serves you well as you create your own dream plan.

If you have taken the time to complete the accompanying workbook or made notes as you read this book, your next step is to summarize your notes into a master plan. Then put your plan in motion by taking the first step. This plan is something that will guide you in the beginning and get you back on track when you experience feelings of loss. It may evolve and adapt as you make your way through your own phases of retirement. Whatever life throws your way, you can use the principles presented here to help you create and enjoy your own happy retirement!

ABOUT THE AUTHOR

Guy Burberry is an independent financial planner who has counselled hundreds of families on the planning and management of their investments. He has an educational background in economics and financial planning with a minor in psychology, and he brings these unique disciplines together to approach retirement planning from a new angle, focusing on the psychological aspects of making the leap into a happy retirement.

Over the past 26 years, Guy has helped many individuals achieve financial independence. Now, his goal is to take this process a step further and guide them through the non-financial aspects of creating a fulfilling retirement.